CW00543990

As a longtime specialist picture researcher, Katie Greenwood has been responsible for the look and success of a host of best-selling and internationally published visual books. With a keen eye for an image, she also has a professional awareness of what illustrators and designers need, and expert knowledge of the history of aesthetics, fashions and colour trends. This is her first book.

YEARS OF COLOUR

BEAUTIFUL IMAGES
& INSPIRATIONAL PALETTES
FROM A CENTURY OF INNOVATIVE
ART, ILLUSTRATION & DESIGN

KATIE
GREENWOOD

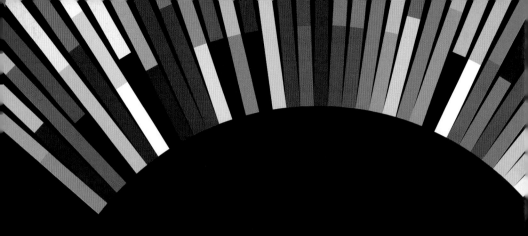

100 Years of Colour

An Hachette UK Company
www.hachette.co.uk

First published in the UK
in 2015 by ILEX, a division of
Octopus Publishing Group Ltd

Octopus Publishing Group
Carmelite House
50 Victoria Embankment
London, EC4Y 0DZ§
www.octopusbooks.co.uk

Design, layout, and text copyright
© Octopus Publishing Group 2015

Publisher: Roly Allen
Senior Specialist Editor: Frank Gallaugher
Senior Project Editor: Natalia Price-Cabrera
Assistant Editor: Rachel Silverlight
Commissioning Editor: Zara Larcombe
Project Editor: Ellie Wilson
Art Director: Julie Weir
Designer: Richard Wolfströme
Senior Production Manager: Katherine Hockley

Katie Greenwood asserts the moral right
to be identified as the author of this work.

ISBN 978-1-78157-284-9

A CIP catalogue record for this book is
available from the British Library

Printed and bound in China

10 9 8 7 6 5 4 3 2 1

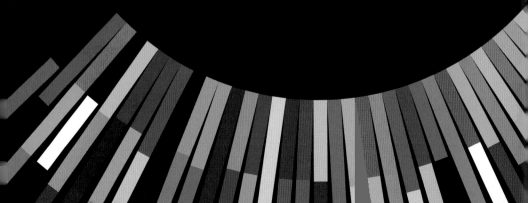

CONTENTS

100 YEARS OF
COLOR

This book is a carefully curated collection of images—a celebration of color, and a visual journey through the 20th century. We will travel from the naturalistic tones of Art Nouveau to the patriotic palettes of World War II, and from the rainbow 1960s to the neon identity of punk and beyond. Color has the ability to visualize change, ideas, and feelings, with certain colors being synonymous with an era or movement. As society shifts between stability and unrest, so color can alternate between the reassurance of tonal harmony and the excitement of a clashing combination. In 100 years, technology revolutionized the way images and objects are created and reproduced, and how we all experience color in our lives today.

One image has been chosen for each year of the century, with five colors selected for the palette, displayed in varying ratios. The sRGB values are included for reference and replication. An introduction to each decade gives some background on color trends and a wider view of what was happening within culture and the arts. The images cover a range of subjects, including fashion, interiors, music, and film, and come from a variety of mass-produced sources, such as posters, magazines, advertisements, wallpapers, and textiles.

My research was not without its challenges and contradictions. Condensing each decade into just 10 images and a brief overview was a hugely reductive exercise, and in addition each image needed to be portrait format, with enough colors available for the palette. Therefore the important red, black, and white combination used extensively in Russian Constructivist graphics, along with other beloved images, fell by the wayside. However, the constraints also led me to images I might not have discovered otherwise, some fitting the expectations of a decade, with others appearing anachronistic—a reminder of color's ability to surprise us.

Reaction to color is a subjective experience and individual interpretations can be as broad as the spectrum itself. I hope the following pages provide interest and inspiration to color lovers and image junkies everywhere.

— Katie Greenwood

As this book is printed using CMYK inks, we can directly convert these colors to RGB values within an sRGB color profile (most useful for web content). However, the exact CMYK values will vary depending on which CMYK color profile your particular printer is using. Toward that end, on pages 230–239, you'll find all the CMYK color values listed according to the three most common CMYK profiles.

1900s

As the new century began, Paris found itself to be the cultural and artistic capital of the world. Fin-de-siècle graphic artists such as Jules Chéret mastered the process of chromolithography and paved the way for the ascension of the advertising poster to a newly found status, mirrored in society by an increasing fashion for collecting ephemera. Chéret's colorful and painterly style encapsulated the spirit of Belle Époque gaiety, as did his female subjects, who joyously promoted the latest spectacle or product. His influence would be far reaching: by elevating the poster to an art form and harnessing the power of color to communicate, and to sell, he revolutionized the urban visual landscape and inspired a new generation of commercial artists and designers.

It was Paris that had seen the movement of Art Nouveau crystallize and become the prominent decorative style of the 20th century, dominating the city's Exhibition Universelle in 1900. Nearly called "Mucha Style" after its chief exponent, the Czech artist Alphonse Mucha, it was in part a visual reaction to increasing industrialization, its principles being aligned to the Arts and Crafts movement in England. The natural world influenced Art Nouveau's style as well as its palette: flora, fauna, and the landscape all informed the fluid, intricate motifs and muted hues that were to be found adorning graphics, fabrics, and the home.

The "new art" had quickly disseminated throughout Europe and beyond in the previous century. Regional offshoots such as the Vienna Succession were established, and American illustrators adopted the flowing line and organic coloring favored by their European counterparts. However, artists including Edward Penfield began to reject the overt decoration of Art Nouveau, abandoning the movement's swirling ornamentation to create a simplified illustration style Limited palettes were fused with bold outlines and flattened planes of color, as influenced by Japanese ukiyo-e prints. The impact of these "pictures of the floating world"—along with other Japanese crafts—was widespread throughout the arts, and can also be seen within the book illustration taken from Denslow's Mother Goose in 1901.

Not all colors were drawn from nature—some came from the imagination. Italian émigré Leonetto Cappiello is often referred to as the "father of modern advertising" for his innovative use of form and color; his bold, often unnaturally toned figures popping from black backgrounds, creating a distinctly modern visual language for the new century. His advertisements for consumer goods such as the Swiss brand Chocolat Klaus were revolutionary at the time for turning the colors of nature on their head, his choice of bright red for the horse preceding the German artist Franz Marc's Expressionist equines by nearly a decade.

Along with the advertising poster, advancements in printing and distribution meant that illustrated magazines were also on the rise, with color plates satirizing society figures and the latest political wrangles, depicting popular music hall and theater stars, and illustrating current fashions. Within their pages, women were often the subjects of figural fantasy, and in 1906 we see the feminine ideal of the Gibson Girl—with her exaggerated and corseted S-curve torso and hair piled high—showing off the latest pastel summer fashions. While this popular archetype was modern in many ways, she would never have joined the burgeoning suffrage movement or demanded voting rights for women. We close with Sadie Wendell Mitchell's *Dig*—rich in jewel-like colors seemingly inspired by the designs of Louis Comfort Tiffany—and a call for women to educate themselves to equality.

IMPRIMERIES CHAIX & DE MALHERBE, ÉDITEURS _ 1900

1900

**Poster for the Exhibition Universelle
in Paris titled *The Weaver***
Artist: Jules Chéret

R	G	B
32	97	137
239	189	88
253	231	172
208	160	146
230	123	92

Book illustration from
Denslow's Mother Goose
Artist: W. W. Denslow

R	G	B
102	96	68
116	126	106
215	147	84
212	189	171
93	49	27

1902

Advertisement for Cycles Perfecta
Artist: Alphonse Mucha

R	G	B
178	62	32
206	139	90
218	185	148
159	101	86
108	115	99

1903

Advertisement for Chocolat Klaus
Artist: Leonetto Cappiello

R	G	B
232	189	39
100	135	97
75	76	127
205	47	23
0	0	0

CHOCOLAT
KLAUS

DELECTA LE SUPRÊME DU GENRE CHOCOLAT *SUISSE*

Imp. P. VERCASSON & Cie 43, Rue de Lancry, PARIS

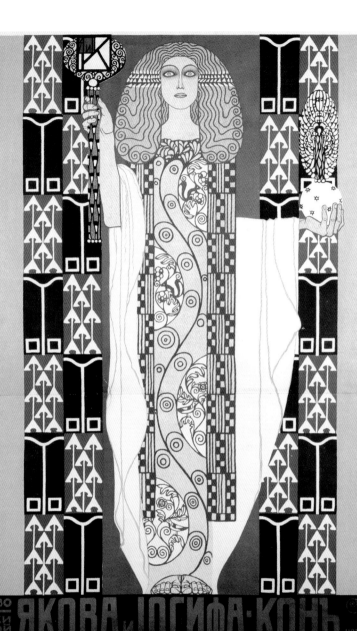

АКЦ.О^{ВО} ФАБРИКИ ВѢНСКОЙ МЕБЕЛИ ⁞ **ЯКОВА и ІОСИФА · КОНЪ** ВЪ НОВОРАДОМСКѢ

ГЛАВНЫЕ СКЛАДЫ ВЪ:

МОСКВѢ, СТ^Б.ПЕТЕРБУРГѢ, ВАРШАВѢ, КІЕВѢ, РОСТОВѢ ^Н/д.

МЕБЕЛЬ ДЛЯ РЕСТОРАНОВЪ
КОНЦЕРТНЫХЪ ЗАЛЪ И ТЕАТРОВЪ
ПОЛНЫЯ ОБСТАНОВКИ СПАЛЕНЬ
СТОЛОВЫХЪ, КАБИНЕТОВЪ И ГОСТИННЫХЪ
СОБСТВЕННЫЯ МАСТЕРСКІЯ ПОДЪ РУКОВОДСТВОМЪ
ХУДОЖНИКОВЪ И ОПЫТНЫХЪ ТЕХНИКОВЪ.

ЛИТОГР. И ТИПОГР. АЛЬБЕРТ БЕРГЕРЪ ВЪНА VII.

1904

**Advertisement for the furnishing company
Jacob and Josef Kohn**
Artist: Koloman Moser

R	G	B
47	45	62
128	109	51
189	32	93
252	226	195
195	192	176

1905

Fabric design
Artist: Eugène Grasset

R	G	B
161	48	45
227	175	168
207	170	144
207	89	36
105	62	35

1906

Fashion illustration from
***The Delineator* magazine**
Artist: Unknown

R	G	B
205	218	189
249	193	168
255	242	172
201	210	149
251	250	228

Wiener Werkstätte postcard no. 15
Artist: Rudolf Kalvach

R	G	B
71	96	141
187	138	47
182	61	23
245	233	205
0	0	0

CORNELL

Copyright 1908
by Chas W. Beck Jr.

1908

Poster for Cornell University
Artist: Edward Penfield

R	G	B
155	61	29
173	134	89
236	222	198
175	166	149
71	63	57

1909

Poster titled *Dig*, part of the artist's
Girls Will Be Girls series
Artist: Sadie Wendell Mitchell

R	G	B
155	45	34
69	108	48
79	126	113
211	134	40
117	65	50

DO IT NOW

THE STUDY OF BUGOLOGY

NATUREFAKERS OF

THE PSYCHOLOGY OF THE MALE HUMAN

SADIE WENDELL MITCHELL

1910s

A number of art movements worked toward the freeing of both color and form, visualizing the emergence of Modernism. The breaking up of space found in Cubism and Futurism and the seemingly boundless palettes of Expressionism, among others, all trickled down and started to shift visual culture toward geometry and an expressive use of color.

We open with a costume design in a flaming palette by the Russian artist Léon Bakst, created for Igor Stravinsky's ballet *The Firebird*. The exotic designs Bakst produced for Sergei Diaghilev's Ballet Russes are significant not only for their application of intense color, abstract pattern, and innovative form—influenced by folk art and Eastern cultures as well as contemporary painting—but also for demonstrating a new synergy between art, fashion, and music.

Bakst's work was a likely influence on the eminent Parisian fashion designer Paul Poiret, who, having cast aside the constraints of both the petticoat and the corset in the preceding decade, would come to dominate *la mode* in the early 1910s. As with haute couture today, his garments were both coveted by bohemian high society and influential on the mass market: featuring exotic fabrics, trimmings, and accessories such as the turban, they inspired a wave of Orientalism.

Through inventive cuts and the application of draping he produced geometric silhouettes such as the lampshade tunic and cocoon coat. His column dresses were straight-sided and often appeared in vivid blocks of flat color, as seen in the 1911 poster advertising a showing in Vienna. This was revolutionary at the time and stood in stark contrast to the corseted, conservative fashions of the Edwardian era. Poiret had helped to free women from restrictive clothing, but also from limited color choices. His attitude to fashion would have likely been shared by the woman seen in the skirt suit promoting *The Suffragette* periodical in 1913.

Whilst the avant-garde shaped the world visually, the old guard continued to mould the political landscape. However, the assassination of an Austro-Hungarian Archduke in 1914 triggered a series of events that would end the Belle Époque and culminate in World War I. Popular graphic artists such as Ludwig Hohlwein in Germany and J. C. Leyendecker in America were employed to produce persuasive propaganda, encouraging men and, for the first time, women to do their duty. The power of design was realized on a mass scale, and the heroic imagery belied the catastrophic reality of nations at war—reflected in somber patriotic and military tones.

By the war's end, the home had became a refuge and a host of interior decoration magazines became increasingly popular, such as the *Ladies Home Journal* and *House Beautiful* in the U.S. Interior design was also influenced by innovation in the arts, with companies such as William Foxton in England commissioning modern artists to create mass-market furnishings. The aim was to raise the standard of design, stimulate the industry within post-War economies, and brighten up domestic life after the dark days of conflict. In 1918 we see a Foxton furnishing fabric designed by the artist Constance Irving, who had exhibited alongside Picasso, Matisse, and Gauguin earlier in the decade. Her abstract botanical design features a harmonious palette of blue, brown, and teal, highlighted by a complementary accent of orange— demonstrating a painterly appreciation of color, as well as a growing cross-pollination between art and everyday living.

The aesthetic innovations and world events of the decade had led to a shift in visual consciousness as well as significant social change. The forward march of Modernism would only gather pace over the coming years, as the relationship between art and commerce went from strength to strength.

1910

**Costume design for the
ballet *The Firebird***
Artist: Léon Bakst

R	G	B
238	127	29
248	177	29
203	125	18
226	96	17
163	48	22

1911

**Advertisement for
Paul Poiret in Vienna**
Artist: Unknown

R	G	B
206	51	79
144	144	94
73	95	118
219	115	130
231	215	199

ZU GUNSTEN DES UNTER HÖCHSTEM PROTEKTORATE
DER DURCHLAUCHTIGSTEN FRAU ERZHERZOGIN MARIA
JOSEPHA STEHENDEN VEREINES „LUPUSHEILSTÄTTE"
UND „I. ÖFFENTLICHES KINDERKRANKENINSTITUT" DES
UNTER DEM HÖCHSTEN PROTEKTORATE DER DURCH-
LAUCHTIGSTEN FRAU ERZHERZOGIN MARIE VALERIE
STEHENDEN „WIENER WÄRMESTUBEN- UND WOHL-
TÄTIGKEITSVEREIN"

27·28·29·NOVEMBER URANIA

PAVL POIRET IN WIEN

1. KINEMATOGRAPH · 2. CONFÉRENCE, GEHALTEN VON
PAUL POIRET · 3. VORFÜHRUNG SEINER NEUESTEN MODE
SCHÖPFUNGEN DURCH MANNEQUINS AUS POIRETS
ATELIER · PROMENADE DER MANNEQUINS IM ZUSCHAUER
RAUM · BEGINN ½4 UHR NACHMITTAGS : PREISE DER
PLÄTZE: 25, 20, 15, 10 U. 5 KRONEN, LOGEN À 120 KRONEN
KARTENVERKAUF BEI ALLEN DAMEN DES KOMITEES
OBIGER VEREINE U. AN DER TAGESKASSE DER URANIA
I. ASPERNPLATZ. TELEPHON 23909 SOWIE BEI KEHLEN-
DORFER I. BEZIRK. KRUGERSTRASSE 3 · TELEPHON 6238

GRAPHISCHE KUNSTANSTALT BRÜDER ROSENBAUM WIEN VIII

1912

Cover for *Red Onion Rag*
music sheet
Artist: Unknown

R	G	B
63	110	74
197	204	180
236	178	168
206	48	24
56	31	19

1913

Poster for *The Suffragette* newspaper
Artist: M. Bartels

R	G	B
242	179	164
207	84	71
145	126	122
232	188	94
141	143	70

ROTE KREUZ-SAMMLUNG
1914
SAMMLUNG ZUGUNSTEN DER FREI-
WILLIGEN KRANKENPFLEGE IM KRIEGE

1914

Poster for the German Red Cross
Artist: Ludwig Hohlwein

R	G	B
118	100	50
174	147	79
225	217	185
131	55	18
0	0	0

1915

Magazine illustration
Artist: H. Rewald

R	G	B
117	107	92
114	56	70
62	87	69
148	138	64
227	210	116

He did his duty.
Will YOU do YOURS?

PUBLISHED BY THE PARLIAMENTARY RECRUITING COMMITTEE, LONDON. POSTER NO. 20.

PRINTED BY JOHNSON, RIDDLE & CO. LTD., LONDON, S.E.

1916

Recruitment poster for the British Army
titled *He Did His Duty. Will You Do Yours?*
Artist: Unknown

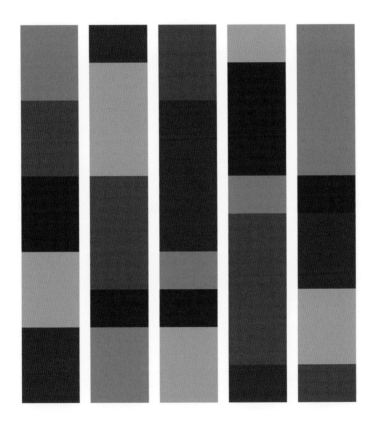

R	G	B
192	143	42
141	93	31
74	60	77
203	173	128
161	53	27

1917

Poster for the U.S. Marines
Artist: J. C. Leyendecker

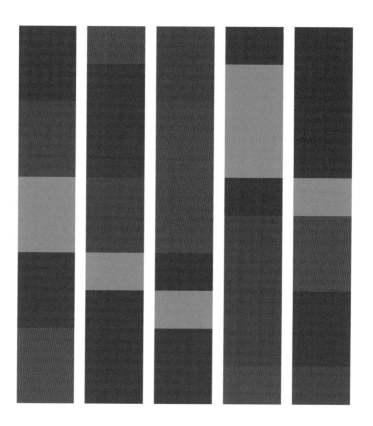

R	G	B
112	93	37
141	99	28
194	155	79
90	92	89
175	95	31

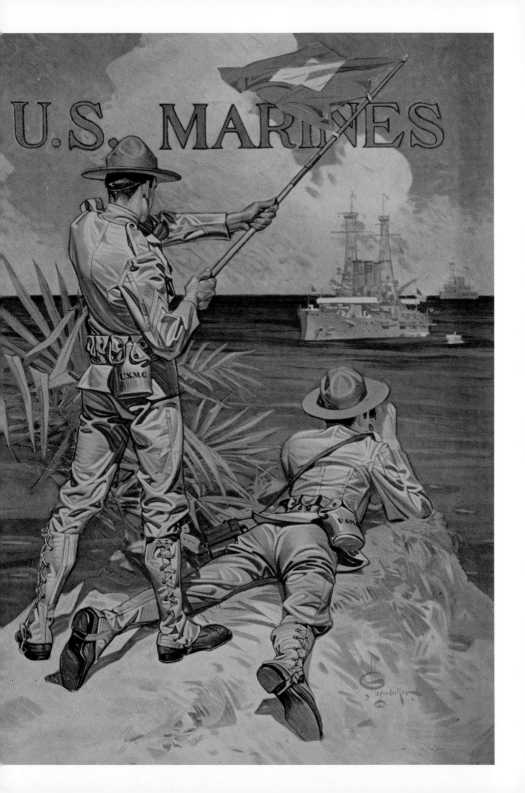

1918

Furnishing fabric
Artist: Constance Irving

R	G	B
144	118	94
83	105	136
189	108	23
139	158	142
40	62	85

1919

Cover for *The House Beautiful* magazine

Artist: Maurice Day

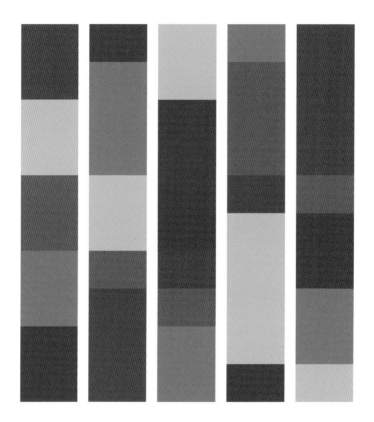

R	G	B
194	63	38
220	193	142
183	94	56
123	136	117
110	80	96

THE HOUSE
BEAUTIFUL

CITY HOUSE *and* APARTMENT NUMBER

25 CENTS   •   NOVEMBER • 1919   •   3.00 a YEAR

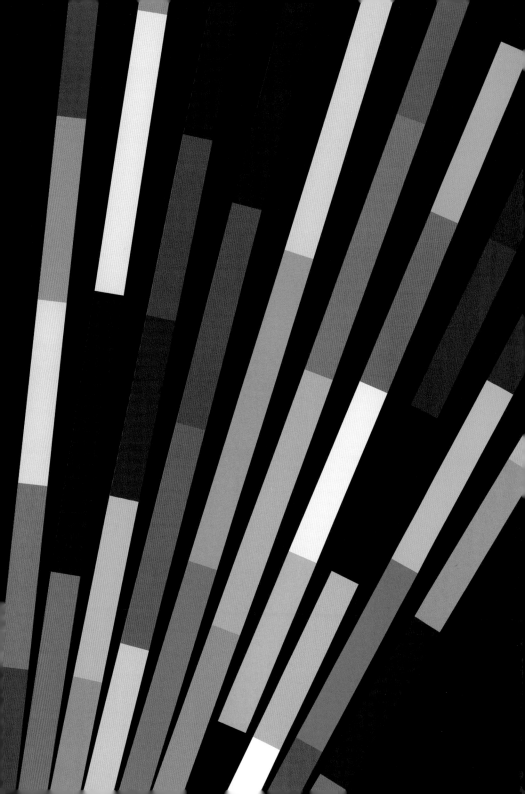

1920s

TThe 1920s were for the young who had seen their parents' generation descend into the horrors of war and were ready for change, and some fun. In terms of color, too, it was a riot; palettes became permeated with the spirit of freedom and frivolity that ran throughout the decade.

Increasingly affordable travel opened up new horizons, and there was a renewed interest in non-Western art forms, bringing exotic bright colors and patterns to the fore. This was accompanied by discoveries about the ancient world, such as the uncovering of Tutankhamun's tomb, and we see images by illustrators like Georges Barbier infused with the deep blues and golds of Egypt. As in previous decades, Eastern motifs and tones were fashionable for their exoticism and sensuality. But along with a desire to move forward, there was nostalgia for cultures that, through the looking glass of history, appeared stable, peaceful, and prosperous.

In 1925 Paris hosted the *Exposition Internationale des Arts Décoratifs et Industriels Modernes*, an exhibition which would both showcase the Machine Age style of decoration popular within the applied arts, and give rise to its name: Art Deco. Georges D'Arcy's Ideas from the same year demonstrates Deco's inclination toward geometric abstraction and use of vivid color. Other art and design movements—such as the Bauhaus, de Stijl, and Constructivism—shared Deco's desire for geometry and strong use of color, but opted for functional minimalism over any form of decoration.

In Britain, transport systems within the city of London were extended and improved as the modern metropolis grew, with London's Underground commissioning British artists to attract travelers to the Tube. We see poster artist Horace Taylor employing a bold use of clashing color in his poster *Brightest London is Best Reached by Underground*—the "anything goes" attitude being applied to color as it was to life.

The institution of the music hall had survived the war, but began to be overtaken by cinema, along with the medium of radio, as a means of mass entertainment. Silent-era movie actors rose to new levels of fame and many new magazines were established or saw their circulations increase as demand for images of Hollywood stars and insights into their lives fused with increasingly efficient methods of production and distribution. It is fitting that *The Jazz Singer* (1927) was the first film to feature synchronized sound and dialog. The new form of music, which had its roots in African-American traditions and supplanted ragtime, would become the soundtrack for the decade and give birth to several scandalous dance crazes such as the Charleston and the Shimmy. In America, the prohibition of alcohol went hand in hand with a loosening of existing social practices, with the flapper—an independent, active, irreverent young woman who drank and danced the night away—becoming a widespread and controversial archetype.

Daughters shocked their parents with increasingly risqué fashions; rising hemlines, exposed flesh, and the heavy use of make up, previously seen as the preserve of prostitutes. Gender boundaries became blurred, with short bobbed hair and the androgynous *garçonne* look becoming popular. This can be seen in the 1926 illustration for a lingerie brand, rendered in the pochoir method, a skilled hand-stenciling technique capable of producing vibrant color. Fashionable colors included deep and medium blues, jade and mint greens, dusty peach, pale yellow, light gray, sand, burnt orange, and purple, with metallics adding a little shimmer to the shimmy. Black also came to the fore with the color no longer being preserved for mourning.

The decade on the move embraced the car as both a means of travel and a status symbol, as manufacturing boomed via the production line technique pioneered by Ford. We close with a vision of the future driven by fossil fuels and big business.

E·Mc·K·K

TOUCAN

| NO | MTs | YDs |

1920

**Label design for texile
company Steinthal**
Artist: Edward McKnight Kauffer

R	G	B
98	97	111
143	165	102
244	214	86
211	121	51
200	59	36

1921

Cover for *Shimmy Foxtrot* music sheet
Artist: A. Krüger

R	G	B
114	46	79
125	163	129
247	225	193
85	35	20
222	111	32

Shimmy Foxtrot

för PIANO 2/ms

av

L. MUSKANTOR

Kompositörens Egendom
för alla Land

A·KRÜGER

THE INDISCRETIONS OF A STAR

PICTURE-PLAY
MAGAZINE

APRIL, 1922
20 Cents

The
Best Magazi
of the Scree

1922

Cover for *Picture-Play* magazine
Artist: Unknown

R	G	B
74	31	60
204	50	69
158	40	29
224	195	91
143	158	173

1923

**Advertisement for department
store Grands Magazins Dufayel**
Artist: Umberto Brunelleschi

R	G	B
228	107	51
34	40	82
206	60	62
167	98	130
222	203	199

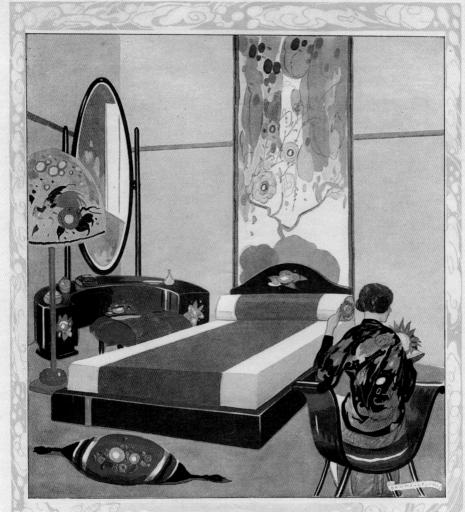

Le Style Moderne

BRIGHTEST LONDON

IS BEST REACHED BY

1924

Advertisement for the London Underground
Artist: Horace Taylor

R	G	B
228	78	105
72	97	158
244	217	86
233	154	68
95	141	92

1925

Design motifs from *Ideas*
Artist: Georges Darcy

R	G	B
190	143	192
136	97	161
209	123	85
237	178	63
138	163	111

a. calavas, paris

MANON
AMOUREUSE

1926

Fashion illustration for lingerie
Artist: Unknown

R	G	B
130	188	147
164	106	170
253	236	197
245	166	128
1	1	0

Cover for *Die Arena* magazine
Artist: John Heartfield

R	G	B
36	48	102
181	44	24
0	0	0
188	186	197
251	250	253

1928

Book illustration from *The Romance of Perfume* titled *Egypt*

Artist: Georges Barbier

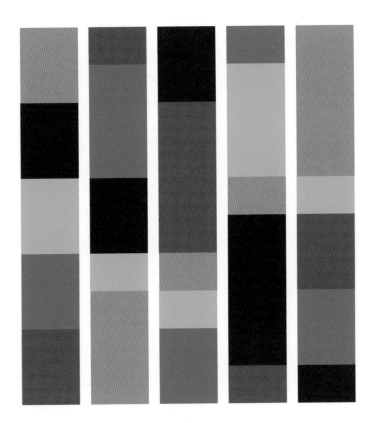

R	G	B
234	143	182
41	50	120
157	201	152
77	126	179
155	109	50

Advertisement for Shell
Artist: Unknown

R	G	B
158	59	46
227	183	79
214	150	70
21	50	65
103	129	135

1930s

The decade saw a dichotomy between the gloom of worldwide economic depression following the Wall Street Crash of 1929 and hope for a better life lived through new technologies, as new materials collided with advancements in style, science, and engineering.

Art Deco would be the design movement that would continue to dominate industrial design and the visual and applied arts. Characterized by streamlining, symmetry, geometric motif, and a rich palette, somewhat darker than in the 1920s, its opulence stood in stark contrast to the financial crisis. Smoky colors, pearlized hues, and metallic finishes were in fashion and mirrored the new architecture springing up in cities around the world. The popularization of the offset-printing process allowed for a greater range of colors, with finer tonality and gradation.

Governments had realized the power of visual communication to disseminate ideas during the First World War and continued to exploit its potential throughout the decade. In Britain, The Empire Marketing Board engaged graphic artists to produce posters promoting colonial goods in order to stimulate trade and build sentiment for imperial policy. Frank Newbould's *The Good Shopper* features the popular colors of rust brown and pine green, with a contrasting accent of pink. Other colors that were in vogue included navy blue, mauve, dark purple, apricot, and teal.

In America, initiatives such as the Work Projects Administration enlisted millions of unemployed Americans to improve the country's infrastructure, providing an income to many who had been affected by the Great Depression. At its peak in 1938, it also left behind a graphic legacy that brought Modernism to a wid-er audience, created by thousands of artists working in the Federal Art Project division. Posters encouraged people to get to work, experience culture, better their health, and visit the newly set up National Parks via improved rail and road networks.

We see WPA artist Shari Weisberg advocating the importance of *Keeping Up With Science* in 1936. Scientific discoveries often fed into design, and in 1935 a crystalline pattern adorns a design for linoleum by the British Silver Studio, a textiles and design firm that created cutting-edge products for the modern mass market throughout the first half of the century.

Hollywood led the style stakes, with screen goddesses favoring floor-length haute couture gowns—such as the pioneering bias-cut designs of Madeleine Vionnet—to create a statuesque silhouette. The decade features two posters for Swedish movie releases: *Dishonored*, featuring Marlene Dietrich, and *ZouZou*, starring Josephine Baker, by the innovative artists Gösta Åberg and Eric Rohman, respectively. Baker had broken ground as a black female entertainer in the 1920s, and in *ZouZou* she became the first to star in a major motion picture, billed as the beautiful "Black Venus."

World's Fairs forecasted a better future for society, with the theme of the New York festival in 1939 being "Building the World of Tomorrow." A souvenir program makes use of the classic Deco motif of the sunburst, the brilliant bright color palette conveying the optimism of the event. The world was looking to the future, but in Europe, signs of unrest had begun to emerge. Fascism took hold of countries such as Germany and Italy, and in Spain General Franco's repression of civilians would culminate in the Spanish Civil War. Alongside the brutality, a host of poster designers such as Amado Mauprivez Oliver produced graphic propaganda for both sides. By the end of the decade, once again competing powers in Europe had set the stage for war and for a return of military inspired palettes.

THE GOOD SHOPPER

B. M. 4. ISSUED BY THE EMPIRE MARKETING BOARD   PRINTED FOR H.M. STATIONERY OFFICE BY WATERLOW & SONS LTD, LONDON, DUNSTABLE & WATFORD

1930

**Poster from the series Empire
Buying Makes Busy Factories titled**
The Good Shopper
Artist: Frank Newbould

R	G	B
180	145	87
243	190	53
112	35	12
81	99	79
198	48	84

1931

Movie poster for *Dishonored (X-27)*
Artist: Gösta Åberg

R	G	B
59	46	61
115	104	102
70	112	107
138	166	160
143	120	143

MARLENE DIETRICH

VICTOR
MC LAGLEN
GUSTAV
SEYFFERTITZ
WARNER OLAND
LEW CODY
BARRY NORTON
REGI: JOSEF VON
STERNBERG

(DISHONORED)
EN FILM FRÅN
PARAMOUNT

MALMÖ-AMSTERDAM-LONDON / PARIS • STOCKHOLM-HELSINGFORS
FLYG MED
A-B AEROTRANSPORT

Advertisement for AB Aerotransport
Artist: Anders Beckman

R	G	B
52	62	86
49	72	108
118	143	165
203	201	188
244	203	42

1933

**Fashion illustration for
Madeleine Vionnet evening gown**
Artist: Jean Demarchy

R	G	B
42	37	35
165	158	163
37	52	105
154	122	70
223	208	188

ZOUZOU
/SVARTA VENUS/
Josephine
BAKER

REGI: MARC ALLEGRET
OFFICIN **ARYSCA**

1934

Movie poster for *ZouZou*
Artist: Eric Rohman

R	G	B
224	48	39
239	124	53
178	124	48
110	164	92
241	242	237

1935

Design for linoleum
Artist: Silver Studio

R	G	B
166	190	169
230	110	102
164	50	54
240	188	205
0	0	0

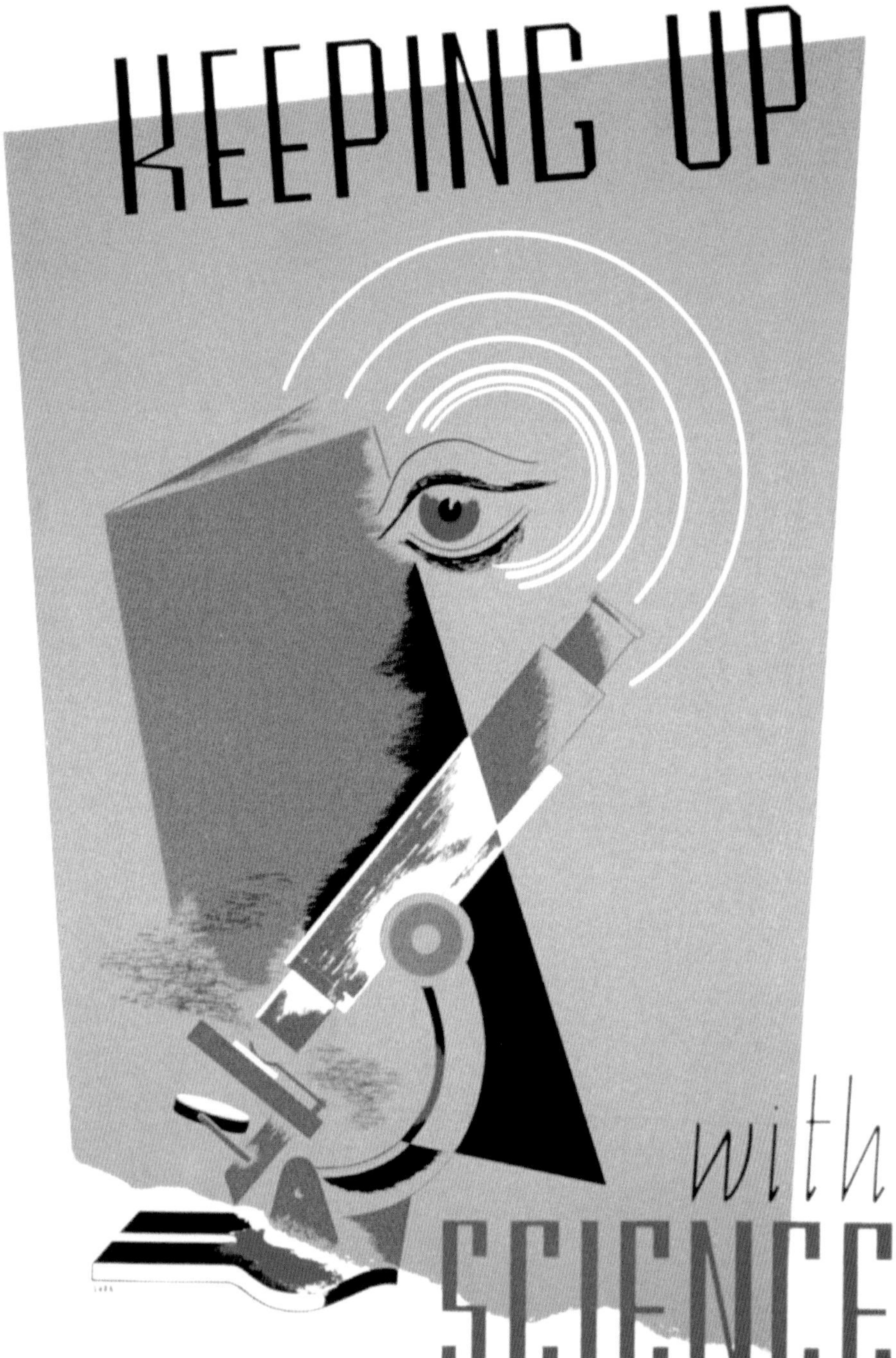
KEEPING UP
with
SCIENCE

1936

**Poster for the Work Projects Administration
titled *Keeping up with Science***
Artist: Shari Weisberg

R	G	B
63	113	183
25	28	59
73	122	147
192	177	125
213	132	106

1937

Political poster titled *The Claw of the
Italian Invader Seeks to Enslave*
Artist: Amado Mauprivez Oliver

R	G	B
244	223	200
167	115	78
154	163	107
129	146	126
222	64	18

JUNTA DELEGADA DE DEFENSA
DE MADRID

DELEGACION DE PROPAGANDA Y PRENSA

LA GARRA DEL INVASOR ITALIANO PRETENDE ESCLAVIZARNOS

SINDICATO PROFESIONALES BELLAS ARTES U.G.T.

RIVADENEYRA C.O.·MADRID.

RANGER NATURALIST SERVICE

HEADQUARTERS
LOOMIS MEMORIAL
AT MANZANITA LAKE

LECTURES
HIKES
MOTOR CARAVANS
CAMPFIRE PROGRAMS
INFORMATION

SEASON
LATE JUNE TO MID SEPTEMB

LASSEN VOLCANIC
NATIONAL PARK

U.S. DEPARTMENT
OF THE INTERIOR

NATIONAL PARK
SERVICE

1938

Poster for the Work Projects Administration
Artist: Unknown

R	G	B
231	198	119
156	108	103
213	181	136
118	95	62
53	52	40

1939

**Cover for the New York World's Fair
souvenir brochure**
Artist: Unknown

R	G	B
245	225	59
137	155	73
105	142	170
230	56	30
233	102	69

NEW YORK
WORLD'S
FAIR

THE WORLD OF TOMORROW

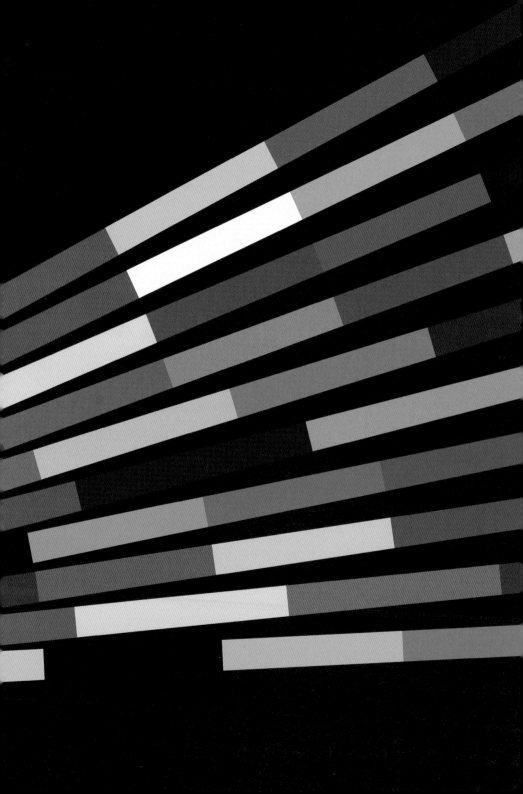

1940s

The Second World War was to dominate the aesthetic of the first half of the decade. Images and fashion were infused by muted military tones with patriotic accents: khaki, brown, army green, navy, and olive, highlighted by the red, white, and blue of the major allied powers.

The production of consumer goods declined as military orders increased. As with the First World War, women played a vital role, stepping up to fill men's shoes on the land, at the office, and in the factories. The hard, manual, and sometimes dangerous, nature of the work was contradicted however by the glamorous promotional propaganda encouraging more women to join the work force. In posters such as Abram Games' 1941 series for the Auxiliary Territorial Service in the UK, we see women poised for duty, hair coiffed and make up flawless— an enduring emblem of the war effort, with the red lip becoming a signifier for the decade.

The pervasive glamor of the time found expression in the pin-up. Images of beautiful women were nothing new, but it was during the war that they proliferated and shifted to a stronger focus on sexuality over beauty. Risqué illustrations by artists such as Art Frahm decorated the lockers of military men, as well as the nose cones of their planes.

Swing's syncopated rhythms would be the backing music to the war. The 1942 MGM musical *Cabin in the Sky* featured some of the greatest singers and musicians of the time: Lena Horne, Ethel Waters, Eddie "Rochester" Anderson, Rex Ingram, Louis Armstrong, and Duke Ellington—an all-African American cast, progressive at a time when some cinemas, especially in the Southern states of America, refused to show movies featuring lead black performers. A colorful Swedish poster brings the movie to life in that year.

When the war ended in 1945 and the austerity began to fade, brighter tones emerged and set the stage for a revolution in color over the coming decades. In 1947, Christian Dior launched his career with his debut collection, which he dubbed "The New Look." The silhouette of a nipped-in waist, broad shoulders and hips, along with a brighter color palette and abundant use of fabric, was a welcome change from the utility of war fashion.

Designer Paul Rand's book on Modernist theory, *Thoughts on Design* (1947), was hugely influential. It advocated the importance of harmony between form and function in design and featured a photogram of an abacus on its cover. The process, often called "cameraless photography," allowed the abacus to be abstracted to its pure form, and Rand used it as the basis for a pattern that would grace textiles produced by L. Anton Maix in New York. The layering of the motif in shades of green and blue enhances the design, allowing for different levels of transparency and intensity. It represents a new era in pattern design when inspiration was taken from everyday objects.

Pulp magazines were popular, but had started to decline in readership by the end of the decade as mass-market paperbacks and comics took over as vehicles for crime, adventure and science fiction stories. Their covers featured brightly colored mastheads and fantastical illustrations, such as Earle K. Bergey's bikini-clad spacewoman on the front of *Thrilling Wonder Stories* in 1948.

A pulp fiction writer is the subject of Carol Reed's haunting film *The Third Man*, set in the chaos of a crumbling post-War Vienna. We close with a French version of its promotional poster which features a high contrast between light and shadow, typical of the Film Noir genre that was popular throughout the decade.

MATCHING THE HATBAND, DUBARRY CRIMSON
LIPSTICK AND PEGGY SAGE FEZ NAIL POLISH

1940

Magazine illustration for Peggy Sage
and DuBarry make-up
Artist: Marcel Vertès

R	G	B
51	61	45
82	113	75
220	198	139
223	55	86
184	45	67

1941

Recruitment poster for the
Auxiliary Territorial Service
Artist: Abram Games

R	G	B
134	118	32
219	153	95
245	238	220
218	45	23
80	140	166

A. GAMES R.E.
JOIN THE
ATS
Abram Games 1941
ASK FOR INFORMATION AT THE NEAREST EMPLOYMENT EXCHANGE OR AT ANY ARMY OR ATS RECRUITING CENTRE
PRINTED FOR H.M. STATIONERY OFFICE BY FOSH & CROSS LTD., LONDON (51/1065)

SVART EXTAS

"CABIN IN THE SKY"

ETHEL WATERS · "ROCHESTER" · LENA HORNE

LOUIS ARMSTRONG
REX INGRAM
DUKE ELLINGTON
och hans orkester
REGI:VINCENTE MINNELLI

1942

Movie poster for *Cabin in the Sky*
Artist: Unknown

R	G	B
37	37	85
85	89	149
91	96	64
248	213	59
159	49	42

1943

War campaign poster
titled *Sew for Victory*
Artist: Pistchal

R	G	B
209	165	27
95	97	47
168	143	84
127	113	74
53	84	87

SEW

FOR VICTORY

SEE MY SECRETARY

1944

Print titled *See My Secretary*
Artist: Art Frahm

R	G	B
51	120	189
107	46	76
123	127	140
198	185	164
152	112	97

1945

Advertisement for Ducharne wool
Artist: Unknown

R	G	B
36	39	84
154	165	162
211	147	141
90	43	31
204	57	29

serglaine
pure wool

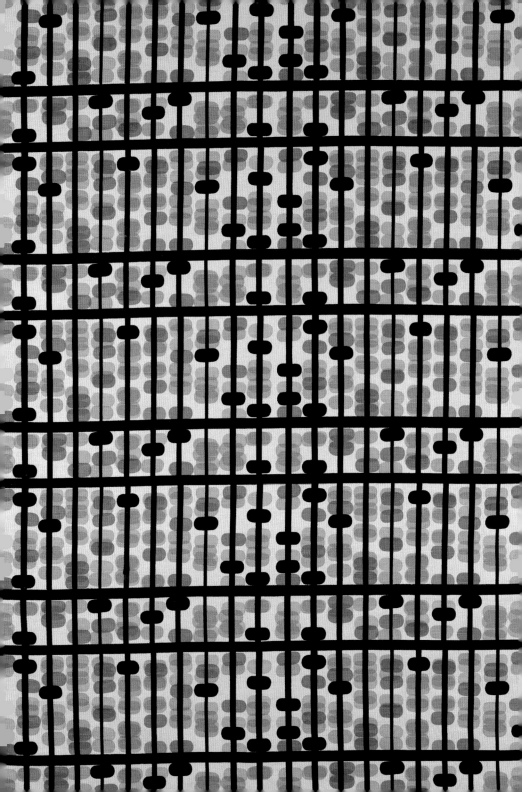

1946

Furnishing fabric titled *Abacus*
Artist: Paul Rand

R	G	B
38	124	140
23	98	138
0	121	75
68	153	68
0	0	0

1947

Fashion illustration for spring collections
Artist: Pierre Simon

R	G	B
127	158	84
86	80	126
243	196	115
204	78	38
153	51	21

NINA RICCI

MARCEL ROCHAS

CHRISTIAN DIOR

Pierre Simon

1948

Cover for *Thrilling Wonder Stories* pulp magazine
Artist: Earle Bergey

R	G	B
42	37	45
76	67	84
210	94	21
254	213	74
230	53	19

1949

Movie poster for *The Third Man*
Artist: Bernard Lancy

R	G	B
201	51	90
101	126	169
147	187	141
25	36	49
230	199	75

ALEXANDER KORDA & DAVID O'SELZNICK présentent UNE PRODUCTION de CAROL REED

JOSEPH COTTEN
VALLI
ORSON WELLES
TREVOR HOWARD

DANS

LE TROISIÈME HOMME

D'après une nouvelle de **GRAHAM GREENE**
Scénario de **GRAHAM GREENE** · CAROL REED et MABBIE POOLE
Réalisation de **CAROL REED**

Filmsonor

b. lancy

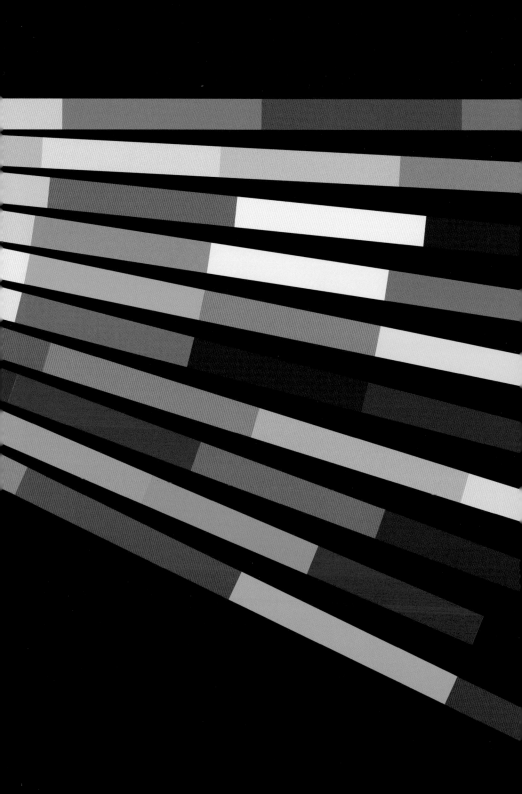

1950s

The transition from war to peace had not been easy, but the Western world became permeated with optimism once more, reflected in lighter and brighter color choices. In the UK, the Festival of Britain of 1951 showcased the country's contribution to science and the arts, and was staged on London's newly built South Bank to visualize the recovery from war. Among the designs were a series of wallpapers and textiles influenced by molecular structures, mirroring new discoveries under the microscope. We see a design by William J. Odell that is based on the atomic structure of nylon. In the early days of the Cold War, the atom was a source of fascination and design inspiration, as well as fear.

Leaps ahead in science and technology fused with a more stable economy to create new lines in consumer goods, packaged and sold via increasingly sophisticated campaigns whose reach was widened by the surge in television ownership.. American advertising agencies—centered on Madison Avenue in New York—dictated tastes and encouraged an unprecedented level of purchasing led by the promise of a better life. Through advertising, women were encouraged back into the role of homemaker with new products and appliances promising to make life easier, and more colorful, such as the Tala kitchen gadgets we see in 1953.

Developments in interior decorating and domestic appliances such as polyurethane paints and new types of plastics opened up a gamut of new shades for the homeowner to play with. Innovation in materials extended to fashion too, with the invention of easy-care fabrics available in more colorways than ever before. Pastels were popular throughout the decade, signifying romance and hope, with pink becoming prominent. They were often bright and combined with primaries—fun was being had with color in the fifties.

Although television rapidly overtook cinema as the dominant form of mass entertainment, Hollywood movies still enraptured their audiences. Saul Bass revolutionized both their title sequences and promotional posters, employing restricted palettes alongside graphic forms to create a unique hand-cut style that's often been emulated. We see a dynamic use of form and type in Giovanni Pintori's designs for Olivetti too, though at the opposite end of the color spectrum, making use of bold primaries with black, a popular mid-century combination.

Following the post-War baby boom, the 1950s saw the birth of the teenager—more affluent and mobile than their parents had been—as well as some of the first prominent youth subcultures in history. There was a backlash against the conformity of mass culture, and movements fueled around music, art, and literature began to emerge, drawing on an increasing sense of alienation from the mainstream. The Beats had their roots in mid-century New York, but the ideals soon spread: a rejection of materialism and everything the American dream represented. Like any youth culture it was ultimately sensationalized and parodied, with the coining of the term "beatnik," racy pulp stories detailing drug-fueled orgies, and major Hollywood releases such as *The Beat Generation*.

As with jazz in the 1920s, black and white musical styles collided to create rock 'n' roll, the increased buying power of its teenage audience feeding its meteoric rise. Elvis—once a provocative symbol of sex and rebellion—became a mainstream icon, appearing in magazines, on television shows, and in numerous Hollywood films, such as the Technicolor Loving You. Through media saturation, what were once subversive youth movements became part of a new mass visual culture that permeated everyday life, and ideas and values became increasingly disseminated through images rather than words.

It makes you want to fall in love!

Endearing
BOURJOIS

Endearing BY BOURJOIS

Endearing Perfume
$1.00, $2.50, $4.50
Eau de Cologne **$1.50**
Dusting Powder **$1.00**
All prices plus tax

THE "ENDEARING" NEW PERFUME
WITH THE PARIS ACCENT!

It makes you _feel_ like a love bird—it makes
him _act_ like a love bird. In fact, our romance
research experts found that 9 out of 10 love
birds choose ENDEARING as the perfume
that "makes you want to fall in love." (The
10th love bird? Completely "carried away"!)

Compounded in Paris . . . Assembled in the U.S.A.

1950

R	G	B
233	171	162
105	139	128
101	93	127
75	150	124
227	213	176

1951

**Nylon wallpaper design
for the Festival of Britain**
Artist: William J. Odell

R	G	B
164	128	73
163	156	94
205	200	184
234	219	195
205	197	143

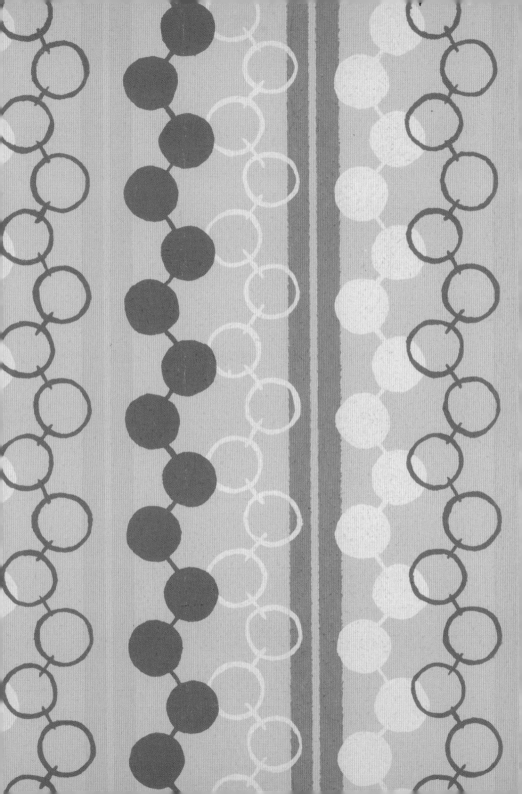

Herne Bay
ON THE KENT COAST

Express trains from London (Victoria) **BRITISH RAILWAYS** ... through trains from the Midlands

For FREE Holiday Guide send 2½ᵈ Stamp to Dept. R.P Council Offices, Herne Bay

PUBLISHED BY THE RAILWAY EXECUTIVE (SOUTHERN REGION) AD 6452   PRINTED IN GREAT BRITAIN BY LEONARD RIPLEY & CO. LTD., VAUXHALL, LONDON.

1952

British Railways advertising poster
for Herne Bay
Artist: Alan Durman

R	G	B
180	24	65
33	64	71
255	233	162
214	100	66
184	206	169

1953

Advertisement for Tala kitchenware
Artist: Unknown

R	G	B
33	34	70
88	136	83
248	237	114
163	154	175
225	211	158

for Beauty and Efficiency

LATEST "TALA" PRODUCTS

Canisters, Cake Boxes, Bread Bins, Kitchen Racks, and Sanicans in White and Red, glossy finish.

"TALA" Icing Set with Plastic turntable that turns at a touch.

"TALA" Icing Pen. Ideal for fine writing and use of coloured icing.

"TALA" Jelly and Aspic Mould Set containing 1 large and 6 small moulds.

"Tala"

COLOURFUL KITCHENWARE
and a "Tala" gadget drawer

makes every Kitchen bright and sparkling, keeps foodstuffs clean and helps you to be an efficient, successful and happy cook. Whenever you wish for a kitchen tool to simplify your work and ease your labours—just ask for "TALA" Kitchenware. On sale at most good class Ironmongers and Stores.

ILLUSTRATED LISTS FROM DEPARTMENT G4, "TALA" WORKS, STOURBRIDGE

Kraftvoll + elegant

54

stauber

ZÜNDAPP *bella*

1954

Matchbox label
Artist: Unknown

R	G	B
246	176	39
244	205	0
243	122	162
104	190	183
247	226	209

**Movie poster for *The Man
with the Golden Arm***
Artist: Saul Bass

R	G	B
24	25	22
40	72	99
64	55	69
173	126	18
226	222	203

FRANK SINATRA · ELEANOR PARKER · KIM NOVAK

THE MAN WITH THE GOLDEN ARM

A FILM BY OTTO PREMINGER · FROM THE NOVEL BY NELSON ALGREN · MUSIC BY ELMER BERNSTEIN · PRODUCED & DIRECTED BY OTTO PREMINGER

Dans la tendance des coloris du Printemps !

Le bas Héllos lance la teinte *"Capucine*

Pour 1956, voici "Capucine" le coloris exclusif que lance HÉLIOS. - "Capucine" s'harmonise avec toutes les nouvelles nuances du printemps. Avec "Capucine" vous êtes à la mode, des pieds à la tête.

Helios BAS - LINGERIE - CHAUSSETTES

1956

Advertisement for Helios stockings
Artist: The Hand

R	G	B
135	123	99
241	224	109
173	191	137
242	121	139
241	72	70

1957

Movie poster for *Loving You*
Artist: Unknown

R	G	B
236	221	117
42	76	62
209	103	80
205	34	39
9	69	109

PARAMOUNT Presents
ELVIS PRESLEY
LIZABETH SCOTT
WENDELL COREY
LOVING YOU
A HAL WALLIS PRODUCTION
TECHNICOLOR®
DIRECTED BY HAL KANTER
SCREENPLAY BY HERBERT BAKER AND HAL KANTER
FROM A STORY BY MARY AGNES THOMPSON

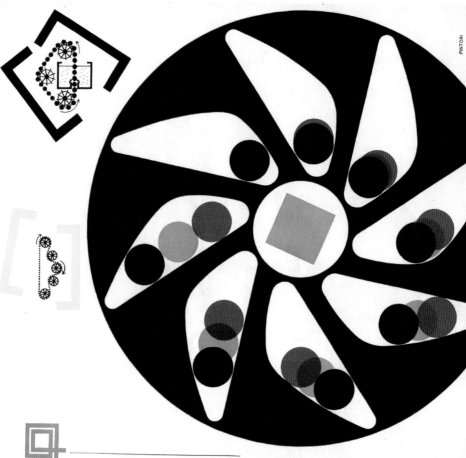

PINTORI

Perpetuum mobile

The diagrams seen above are samples of man's efforts through twenty-odd centuries to achieve perpetual motion. Scorned by science, they nonetheless symbolize a truth: that the human mind, ceaselessly striving for knowledge and progress through research and imagination, is the only true perpetual motion machine.

Olivetti and its machines are products of this striving.

olivetti

Olivetti printing calculators

have won world-wide favor by their speed, ease of operation and dependability; more than half a million have been sold. They offer many unique advantages (Olivetti made the first fully automatic printing calculator, today makes the only one with two registers).

Among the thirteen adding, calculating and accounting machines now offered by Olivetti, there is usually one that fits a particular job as if made to order. Olivetti also offers electric, standard and portable typewriters and the first proportional-spacing manual typewriter.

For information write **Olivetti Corporation of America**, 375 Park Avenue, New York 22, N. Y. Other Olivetti branches in Chicago, Kansas City, San Francisco, Los Angeles.

1958

Advertisement for Olivetti
titled *Perpetual Motion*
Artist: Giovanni Pintori

R	G	B
0	0	0
242	17	16
54	163	25
41	178	249
255	239	6

1959

Movie poster for *The Beat Generation*
Artist: Unknown

R	G	B
255	220	0
120	85	126
111	190	109
228	68	26
239	130	106

1960s

The sixties saw a revolution in color and culture, as the crack that had appeared between the generations in the 1950s widened into a canyon by the end of the decade. Highly saturated hues, made possible by new chemical dyes and inks, were thrown together in wild combinations —in keeping with the pop and psychedelic trends that were to dominate youth culture, and echoing the rebellious sentiment that ran throughout the decade.

In 1963, the Beatles released their first studio album and Beatlemania gripped the world—the hysteria of their young, predominantly female fans unprecedented for any band that had gone before. Intense color is used to promote their UK tour of the same year, with posters such as this designed to grab attention from a distance.

Pop culture infiltrated the art world, with artists such as Andy Warhol incorporating everyday objects and themes of consumerism and the cult of celebrity in their work, rendering them on canvas in clashing polychromatic color. Pop Art influenced interiors and fashion with designers embracing its bold colors and motifs such as the flower. We see a stylized floral furnishing fabric in a fashionable green and blue colorway in 1964. The flower became a symbol of a growing call for peace, as non-violent opposition to the threat of nuclear war and intervention in Vietnam gained ground.

Horizons were widened, as the war in ideology between communism and capitalism instigated a competition between the Soviet Union and United States to dominate spaceflight. We start the decade with a poster encouraging Soviets to "Conquer the Cosmos!," and while Yuri Gagarin became the first human being to orbit the earth in 1961, it was the U.S. that would ultimately win the space race by landing on the moon in 1969. The fight for the final frontier inspired metallic finishes and cosmic designs, but it was not the only thing that was far out about the 1960s.

In 1967 the world went psychedelic, with San Francisco becoming the mecca for the countercultural hippie movement as thousands of "flower children" came to experience its cornucopia of sex, drugs, and rock 'n' roll, during what would come to be termed the Summer of Love. Kaleidoscopic colors and undulating patterns, evocative of an acid trip, influenced artists and designers, as did Art Nouveau, its fluid styling lending itself perfectly to the new psychedelia. Artist Bonnie MacLean produced a number of promotional designs for the legendary Fillmore Auditorium. Her mystical music poster for the English rock band Cream being a fine example of her interpretation of the movement's sweeping organic motifs, rendered in saturated, vibrating color. Art Deco was also revived at the end of the decade and in Milton Glaser's 1968 poster of Aretha Franklin, produced as an insert for the short-lived *Eye Magazine*, he makes use of Machine-Age geometry and typography in popular colors of the decade: deep purple, mid blue, and burnt orange. Franklin, along with other black artists such as those on the Motown and Stax Records labels, provided a soundtrack to the Civil Rights Movement in America. African-Americans campaigned against segregation and inequality, and asserted that black was beautiful, valid, and powerful.

It was a decade of revolution and protest: against racism, the Vietnam War, nuclear weapons, sexism, and homophobia, with color signifying the shifts in society. Color photography became more common with consumers and was increasingly used to document both special occasions and everyday moments, altering the way life was recorded. By the end of the sixties, the transformations in culture—and color—had changed everything.

ПОКОРИМ
КОСМОС!

1960

Propaganda poster titled
Conquer the Cosmos!
Artist: Unknown

R	G	B
47	42	10
76	66	139
164	139	159
242	121	47
128	64	37

1961

Movie poster for *Breakfast at Tiffany's*
Artist: Lutz Peltzer

R	G	B
244	154	67
34	129	64
0	132	166
221	71	145
0	0	0

PARAMOUNT ZEIGT

Audrey Hepburn

Frühstück bei Tiffany

PELTZER

GEORGE PEPPARD · PATRICIA NEAL · BUDDY EBSEN

MARTIN BALSAM UND MICKEY ROONEY

Regie: BLAKE EDWARDS · Produktion: MARTIN JUROW und RICHARD SHEPHERD
Drehbuch: GEORGE AXELROD · Nach dem Roman von TRUMAN CAPOTE · Musik: HENRY MANCINI

TECHNICOLOR

Faites comme moi...

...roulez heureux, **EN TOUTE SÉCURITÉ**

avec

BOUGIE	isolant "SAVOIE"
"FANTASTIC"	Virages et Brouillard
"FULGOR"	Avertisseur de Route
TRICO BRAS-RACLEURS LAVEUR DE PARE-BRISE	Visibilité intégrale

Notices franco - B. P. 111 - Neuilly-s-Seine

6 FOIS CHAMPION DU MONDE   **MARCHAL**

1962

Advertisement for Marchal headlamps
Artist: Unknown

R	G	B
139	197	234
0	0	0
243	234	103
288	77	70
122	66	129

1963

**Concert poster for the Beatles at the Odeon,
Weston-Super-Mare**
Artist: Unknown

R	G	B
27	50	38
56	64	107
244	172	195
233	73	102
254	230	0

1964

Furnishing fabric titled *Watermeadow*
Artist: Coleen Farr

R	G	B
53	140	165
97	166	178
176	188	124
115	130	66
0	124	108

1965

Poster titled *Peace for the world!*
Artist: Karakashev Vilen Surenovich

R	G	B
231	95	29
239	177	34
240	204	49
136	137	143
221	100	118

МИРУ-МИР

1966

Advertisement for Connie shoes
Artist: Unknown

R	G	B
215	38	50
73	165	197
255	209	84
45	104	149
145	194	77

1967

Concert poster for Cream at Fillmore
Auditorium, San Francisco
Artist: Bonnie MacLean

R	G	B
229	54	17
85	38	132
132	95	19
117	41	91
189	170	75

1968

Poster for *Eye Magazine* titled *Aretha*
Artist: Milton Glaser

R	G	B
94	68	126
53	79	150
49	111	140
232	65	48
220	172	84

1969

Concert poster
Artist: Efim Semenovich Tsvik

R	G	B
253	217	71
189	78	44
99	80	103
61	156	199
209	115	133

Гастроли в СССР
ФРИДРИХШТАДТ
ПАЛАСТ
Берлин ГДР
ГОСКОНЦЕРТ СССР

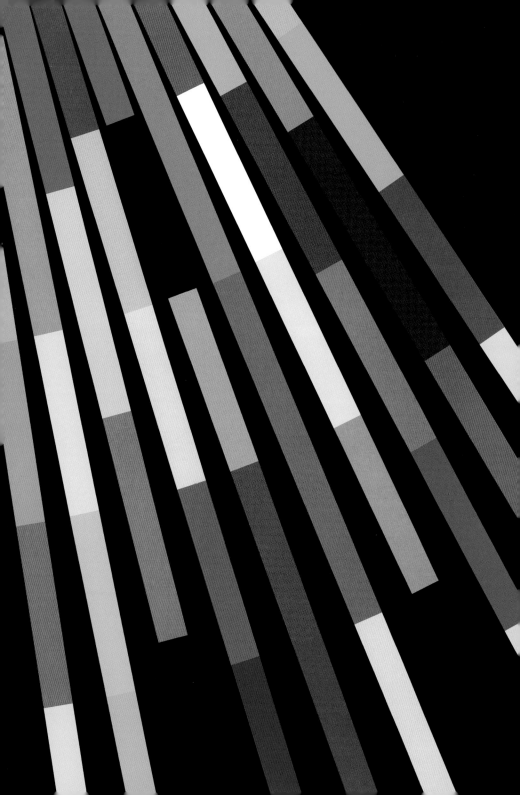

1970s

The swirling psychedelia of the late 1960s didn't end when the new decade began, as the cover of a program for the 1970 Isle of Wight Festival testifies—the hallucinatory motifs are repeated and arranged like a kaleidoscope in rainbow colors. Throughout the seventies, society and design pulled between harmony and discordance, as did its color preferences. A world energy crisis caused environmental concern and created a burgeoning green movement. Natural materials and colors were fashionable for a time, with earthy browns, avocado green, and harvest gold all popular. However, not everyone was interested in going "back to nature," and it wasn't uncommon for an entire outfit or room to be covered top to toe, or floor to ceiling, in eyewateringly bright hues—as seen in the intense red, pink, and purple 1971 wallpaper.

A blacklight poster featuring Isaac Hayes promotes the release of *Wattstax* in 1973. The documentary chronicled the music festival arranged by the Stax record label, hailed as the African-American equivalent of Woodstock. Developed in the sixties, the glow-in-the-dark poster uses inks containing phosphors that fluoresce under the ultraviolet rays emitted from black lights. Fluorescents lent themselves to radical movements, with unnatural colors finding a natural home within punk later in the decade.

Californian counterculture continued to be influential worldwide, and following on from the popularity of surf culture, skateboarding took center stage during the decade. The sport was pushed to new heights after drought and ensuing water restrictions left concrete swimming pools empty, providing a new urban playground for skaters. Artist Jim Evans immortalizes Stacy Peralta, one of the scenes superstars, in 1976. His advertisement for the first World Professional Skateboard Championships makes use of vivid colors, reminiscent of a sunset in the Sunshine State, with his mastery of the popular airbrush technique allowing for a soft gradation of color.

The airbrush is also used to fine effect in a collaboration between some of the greats of rock poster design in 1975: Randy Tuten, Stanley Mouse, Alton Kelley, and the Crazy Arab. Promoting the Rolling Stones' first tour with new guitarist Ronnie Wood, the poster's striking palette with metallic gold ink conveys the extravagance and theatricality of the performance.

The 1970s are significant in terms of the sheer number of musical styles on offer, often standing in direct opposition to each other in terms of their associated ideals—and affinities to color. Studio 54 opened in New York in 1977 and, along with the release of the influential film *Saturday Night Fever* in the same year, bought glamorous disco into mass consciousness. Disco was associated with soft colors, as though seen through dry ice, and pearlized and metallic finishes which sparkled under the club lights.

The year 1977 also saw the punk movement explode, coinciding with the release of *Never Mind the Bollocks, Here's the Sex Pistols*. Punk was in every way the antithesis to disco, politically subversive in its ethos and favoring the color black highlighted by glaring fluorescents. A DIY cut-and-paste aesthetic was seen in punk fashion and was also used by artists such as Jamie Reid, reflecting the raw and anarchic subject matter of the lyrics. Punk graphics became part of a wider experimentation in design that formed a total break from Modernism, mixing media and type weights and shifting focus to personal expression over functionalism—some of the hallmarks of Postmodernism. A New Wave had crashed upon the shore of design.

1970

**Cover for the Isle of Wight
Festival programme**
Artist: David Fairbrother-Roe

R	G	B
299	23	121
238	229	51
229	42	34
116	185	94
140	192	233

1971

Wallpaper titled *Monte Carlo*,
Parisienne*, or *Neon
Artist: Tony Fraser

R	G	B
229	204	207
185	24	23
209	76	137
112	32	69
187	135	181

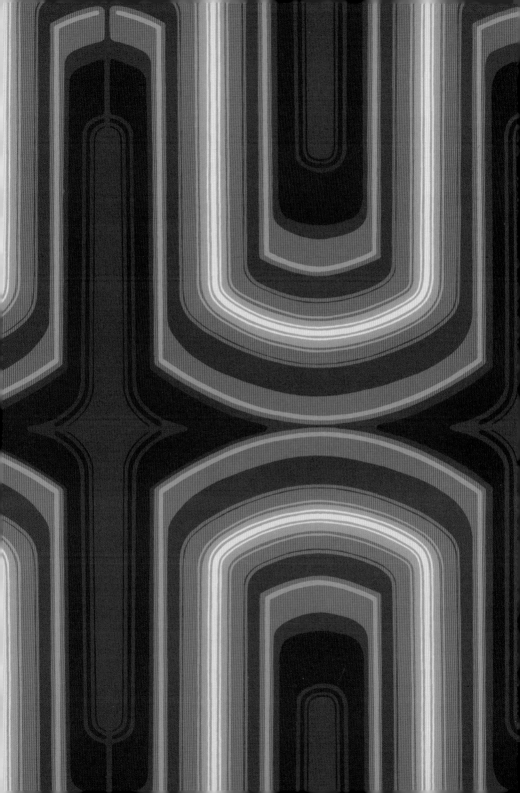

1972

Advertisement for Yost's department store
Artist: Hilgers

R	G	B
242	228	77
36	106	140
230	114	55
152	68	40
123	186	80

1973

Movie poster for *Wattstax*
Artist: Unknown

R	G	B
0	0	0
243	146	76
247	236	108
255	255	255
224	69	145

WATTSTAX

ombre~crème pour les paupières
GUERLAIN

1974

Advertisement for Guerlain cosmetics
Artist: Nikasinovich

R	G	B
198	110	148
145	173	126
236	221	196
187	113	59
124	138	173

1975

Concert poster for the Rolling Stones
at Cow Palace, San Francisco
Artist: Randy Tuten, Stanley Mouse, Alton Kelley
& Crazy Arab

R	G	B
213	41	22
145	89	58
212	173	53
0	0	0
0	118	164

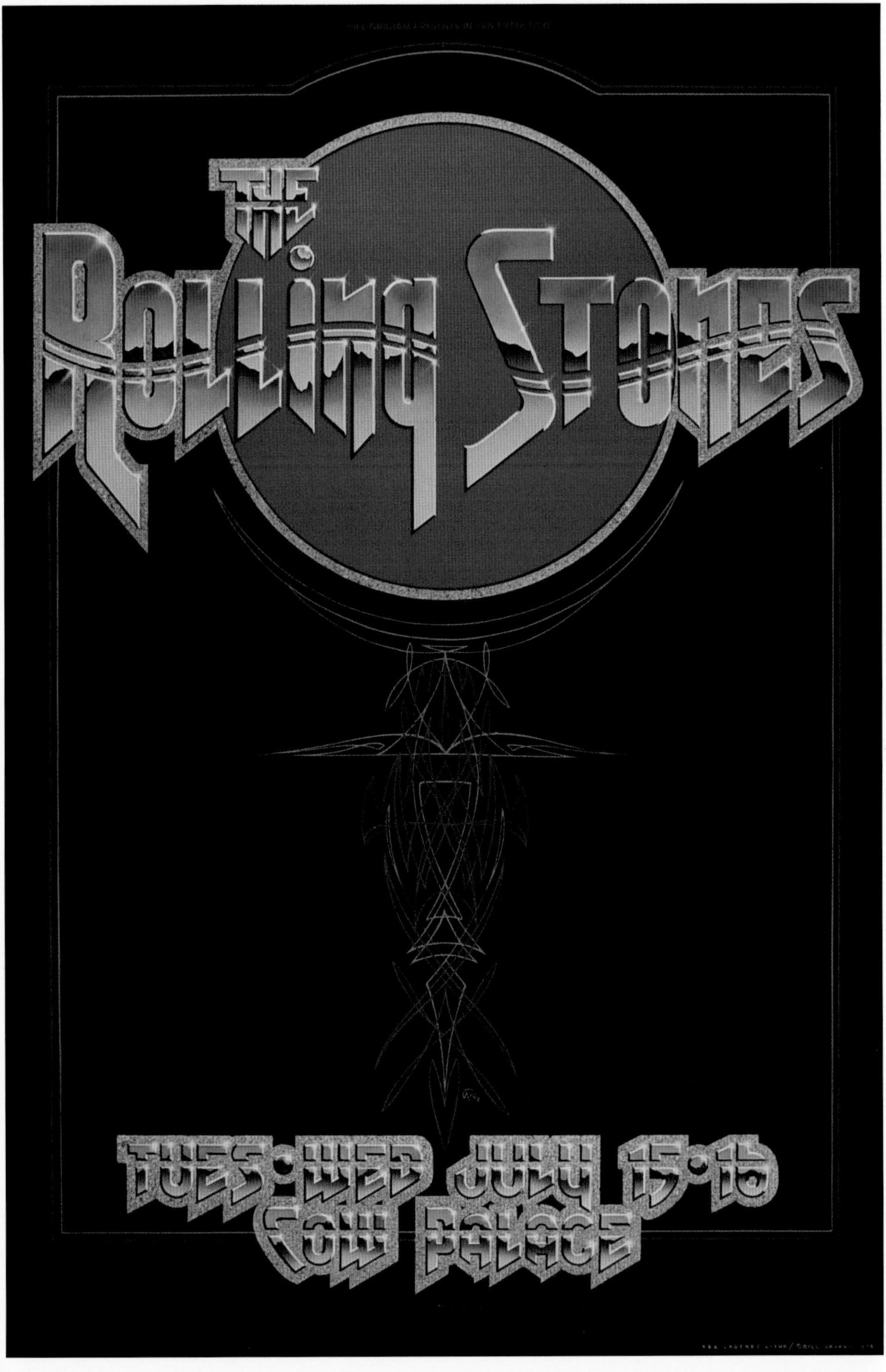
THE
ROLLING STONES
TUES • WED JULY 15•16
COW PALACE

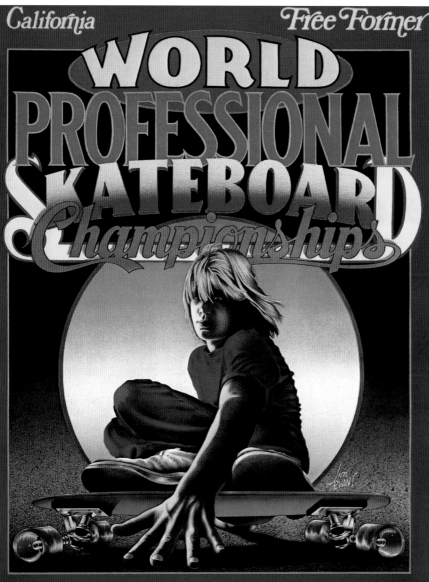

California   Free Former

WORLD PROFESSIONAL SKATEBOARD
Championships

 $20,000 INVITATIONAL

SEPT. 4 & 5 LONG BEACH ARENA 2-8 PM

FLASH CADILLAC AND THE **CONTINENTAL KIDS BOTH NITES**

PRODUCED BY THE PROFESSIONAL SKATEBOARD ASSOCIATION
SANCTIONED BY THE WSA AND PSA RULES BY THE PSA

FREESTYLE, SLALOM, SPEED RACING, HIGH JUMP, BARREL JUMP, HOT DOG AERIALS, SPECIAL SAFETY CLINICS, CONSECUTIVE 360's

TICKETS AVAILABLE AT LIBERTY, TICKETRON AND MUTUAL AGENCIES
Tickets $3.50 in advance, $4.00 day of show   Kids under 12 $2.00 (at door only).

PRESENTED BY WOLF AND RISSMILLER CONCERTS   Ticket Information (213) 437-2255

1976

**Advertisement for
The California Freeformer World
Professional Skateboard Championships**
Artist: Jim Evans

R	G	B
38	56	137
146	89	159
255	223	36
251	191	19
229	36	40

1977

Poster for *Never Mind the Bollocks
Here's the Sex Pistols* by the Sex Pistols
Artist: Jamie Reid & Cooke Key Associates

R	G	B
235	92	130
5	5	6
236	96	67
238	187	35
218	209	122

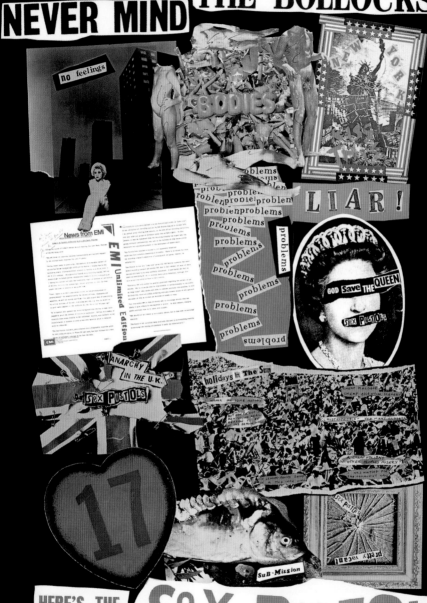

1978

R	G	B
133	196	220
171	207	151
237	231	108
239	143	98
227	139	164

1979

Poster titled *Meet the Cramps*
Artist: X3 Studios

R	G	B
237	233	122
235	94	52
84	171	209
133	193	115
233	77	122

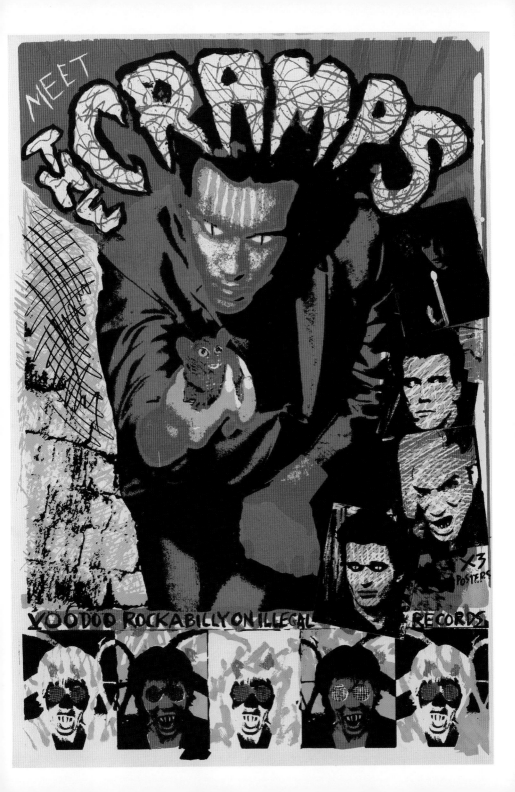

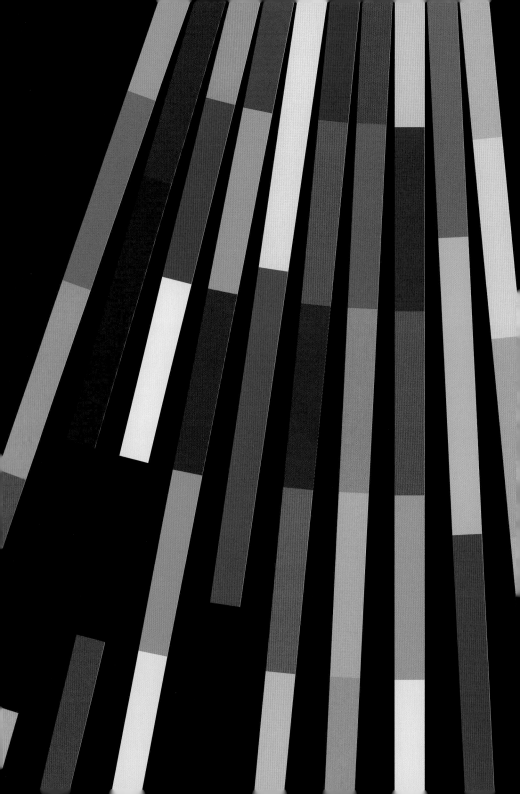

1980s

The eighties experienced intense economic growth and strong colors dominated, particularly red—the color of power, and sex. Color television was to penetrate every home during the decade, with American cable television station MTV bringing music videos to huge audiences, influencing the way teenagers dressed. Michael Jackson's iconic red leather jacket worn in *Thriller* became widely emulated as the height of cool. In 2011 it sold at auction for $1.8 million.

These were neon years, with the fluorescents that had risen to prominence within the subcultures of the seventies becoming widespread, along with shades of aqua, emerald green, magenta, hot pink, cyan, and yellow. Softer pastel tones, like those seen in the cover illustration by Seymour Chwast of the iconic Push Pin Studios, provided a rest for the eye, especially in interior design. We see pastels working with desaturated primaries in the 1983 Havana furnishing fabric by Susan Collier and Sarah Campbell.

New computerized color palettes emerged, mirroring the technological developments that revolutionized the way people communicated, worked, and played. The first half of the decade saw the release of the world's first commercially available cell phone. Musicians embraced electronic technology and a new club culture was born. The pivotal British band New Order fused dance music and post-punk genres, with designer Peter Saville creating an instantly recognizable visual identity for the group. Computer consoles brought digitally generated color out of the arcades and into the home, and were hugely influential on a young and upwardly mobile generation— the bright colors in fashion at the time can be traced to games such as *Pac-Man* and *Tron*, both released for the Atari 2600 in 1982.

Computers also began to be used as a design tool, with Apple releasing its original Macintosh in 1984. Pioneering designer April Greiman embraced the new technology, her layered poster for the exhibition Pacific Wave in 1987 referencing the method of its creation with the use of pixelated type and degenerated imagery. The poster also demonstrates how designers had broken from the grid structure and began to use kinetic, expressive typography, sometimes teetering on the edge of legibility. Type was placed on curves and at angles, and created bold forms such as the stair step seen in a 1987 Italian advertisement for Swatch. Swatch watches were one of the most ubiquitous fashion accessories of the eighties, available in a huge range of colorways and designs, reflecting the trend for personalization within fashion.

As some designers broke the rules, others continued to strive for clarity and simplicity. Japan experienced a rapidly growing economy and was the source of much of the new technology flooding Western markets. Japanese culture was highly influential on Western design and there was a growing synergy between East and West. In graphic design, Ikko Tanaka uses a rigid grid and Modernist geometry to create a traditional symbol of Japan. His simplified geisha, rendered in fields of contemporary color, graces his famous 1981 poster for Nihon Buyo at UCLA.

The Japanese influence is apparent in the ninja-like breakdancers appearing on a 1984 promotional poster for *Beat Street*. The movie starred some of the biggest names in the New York hip-hop scene, and along with *Wild Style*, helped to export the music and culture worldwide. Hip hop's visual expression was graffiti, a reclamation of the urban landscape in vivid spraycan color. It influenced fashion, with designers such as Stephen Sprouse adopting graffiti-like prints in bold colors for their collections. His trademark lettering appears on a poster for *Interview* magazine at the end of the decade.

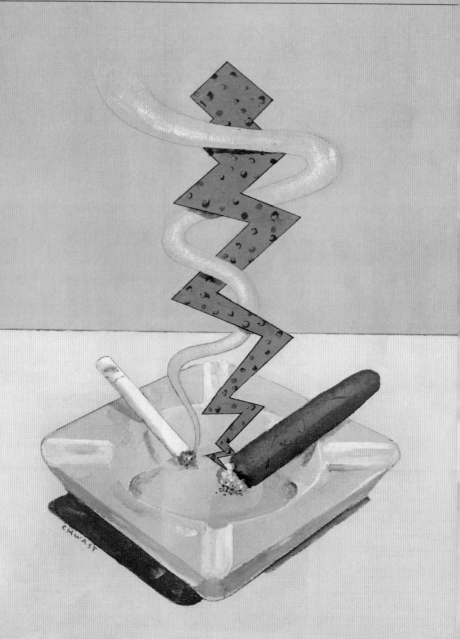

1980

Cover for *Push Pin Graphic* magazine
titled *Couples*
Artist: Seymour Chwast

R	G	B
117	123	152
160	185	197
145	181	135
236	211	123
222	176	161

1981

Poster for Nihon Buyo
Artist: Ikko Tanaka

R	G	B
193	33	37
159	98	165
52	79	158
92	195	221
33	129	112

Nihon Buyo

UCLA
Asian Performing Arts
Institute 1981

Los Angeles
Washington, D.C.
New York

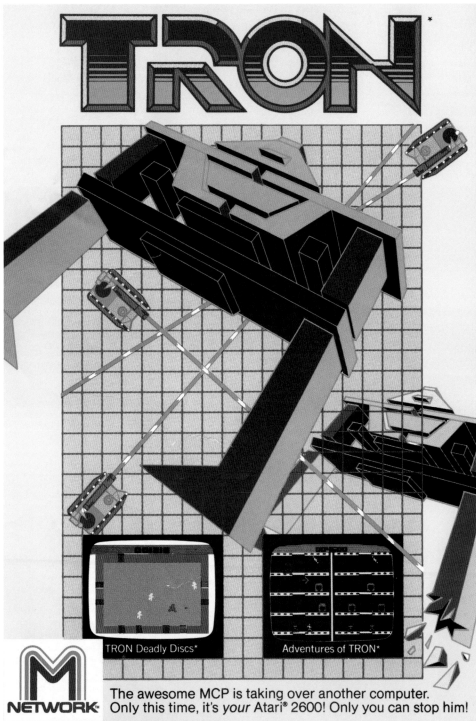

TRON Deadly Discs*

Adventures of TRON*

The awesome MCP is taking over another computer. Only this time, it's *your* Atari® 2600! Only you can stop him!

1982

Advertisement for the computer game *Tron*
Artist: Unknown

R	G	B
244	235	112
99	173	183
216	61	139
55	51	139
237	196	95

1983

Furnishing fabric titled *Havana*
Artist: Susan Collier & Sarah Campbell

R	G	B
229	153	148
238	175	53
148	152	144
97	103	159
180	78	42

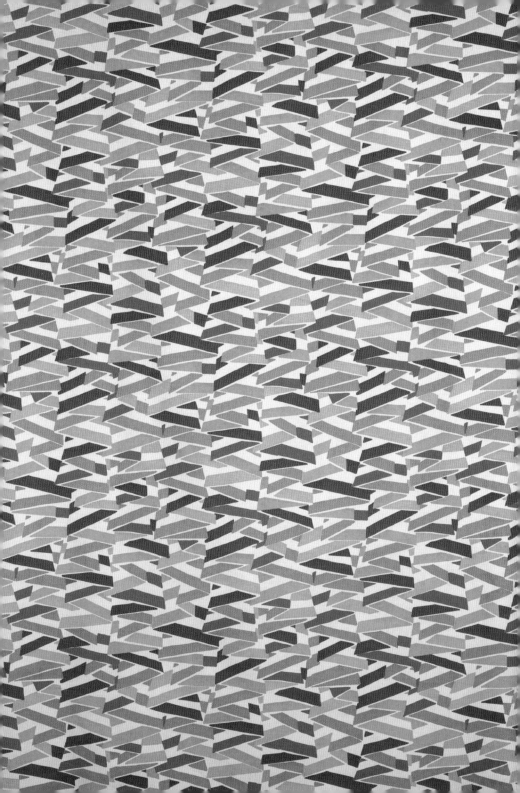

1984

Movie poster for *Beat Street*
Artist: Unknown

R	G	B
239	195	17
234	83	70
64	83	47
206	70	132
63	54	140

1985

R	G	B
188	38	38
49	131	94
0	0	0
61	89	163
229	213	198

PARASOL PACIFIQUE
DE ROCHAS

Maquillage
Printemps-Eté 85

1986

Advertisement for Swatch watches
Artist: Unknown

R	G	B
236	232	117
68	164	131
119	43	102
93	167	206
225	13	39

1987

Exhibition poster for *Pacific Wave*
at the Fortuny Museum, Venice
Artist: April Greiman

R	G	B
225	41	106
0	0	0
252	235	67
31	76	154
239	125	73

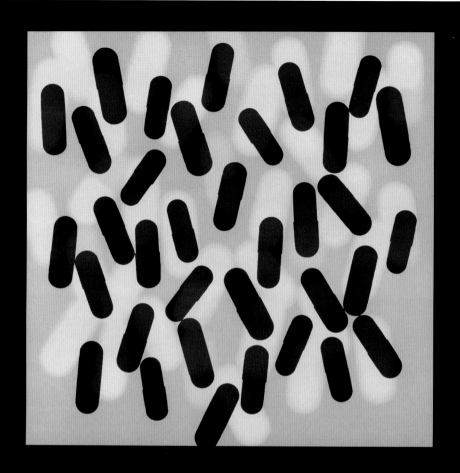

Neworder

Fine time Twelve-inch Maxi-single
from the Lp *Technique*

1988

Poster for *Fine Time* by New Order
Artist: Peter Saville Associates (Design)
Trevor Key & Peter Saville (Image)

R	G	B
140	22	42
232	178	46
0	0	0
63	34	88
151	20	72

1989

Poster for *Interview* magazine
Artist: Stephen Sprouse

R	G	B
0	0	0
232	57	87
242	145	74
6	120	171
90	167	69

Andy Warhol's. *Interview*

JODIE FOSTER

SPROUSE

Photography: Brigitte Lacombe

20 YEARS

1990s

Strong, vivid colors continued to be popular in the nineties, especially within an ever-expanding rave culture, but the early part of the decade also saw a kickback against the showy consumerism of the 1980s, in line with a worldwide recession. Grunge music came to prominence—rebellious and angst-ridden, it was in many ways a continuation of punk, but dressed down. Grunge fashion favored second-hand clothing and a messy, unstyled look in muted tones. Graphic designers mirrored the dirty, layered aesthetic of grunge in their work, with layouts finding affinity with the distortion and feedback of the guitar sound. The desktop computer liberated them from past constraints by speeding up the design process and not requiring ink to visualize ideas.

David Carson was a pioneer of a new kind of typography in which personal expression of the content sometimes won out over legibility. His iconic magazine *Ray Gun* pushed boundaries and inspired a new generation of designers with its unique, refreshing style, resonating with the restless mood of the time. The cover of the premiere issue is seen in 1992.

The capabilities of computer aided design and ideas around deconstruction and clarity were being explored. In 1993 we see Neville Brody's concept for the rebranding of the Deutsches Schauspielhaus theatre in Hamburg that investigates the point at which order becomes chaos. Employing the OCR typeface that was designed for legibility within computer systems, the layered type and symbols come together in a harmonious gray and green color palette.

There is an absence of color in a 1996 poster from John Maeda's digital typographic series *Morisawa 10*, an experiment to improve the legibility and quality of typography. In omitting color, his intention for the focus to be on the form of the four Kana letters "mo," "ri," "sa," and "wa" is enforced. A pioneer in both graphic design and computer science, Maeda fused the disciplines, bringing his knowledge of computer programming to design and vice versa.

Advancements in computer programs made 3D modeling possible, and vector illustrations allowed images to be scaled to any size without loss of quality, giving a pristine appearance. Me Company's promotional poster for Bjork's 1995 single *Army of Me* sees the singer rendered in candy colored 3D as Osamu Tezuka's iconic character Astroboy—the motifs and colors of Japanese manga and anime being popular in design.

The decade saw the birth of the internet, email communication, and widely available pocket-sized cell phones—the world was becoming increasingly connected, changing the very fabric of society. Information and images, from many different cultures and points in history, were to become instantly accessible. The eclecticism and pluralism of the decade is mirrored in the mixing and sampling prominent in dance and hip-hop music, and there was trend for recycling retro styles and colors. In 1998 we see street artist Shepard Fairey's *Viva la Posse* referencing the iconic image of Che Guevara and the posters of revolutionary Cuba. This image formed part of a sticker campaign, which worked to elevate Fairey's company Obey to cult status, with street culture becoming hugely influential on culture at large.

The rapid ascent of an increasingly virtual world, the elevation of the computer, and the spectrum of digital color available at the dawn of the millennium provided an access to information and a freedom of expression unthinkable at the beginning of the century. Yet as with Art Nouveau, technological advancements and their effect on everyday life can also lead to a desire to seek out the colors of nature. Today, designers are equipped with a limitless digital palette and the technology to instantly reference historic and cultural trends. Color choices are infinite, but drawing on just 100 combinations seen in the last century, hopefully this book has provided a starting point for inspiration.

1990

Fabric titled _Nimbus_
Artist: Georgina von Etzdorf

R	G	B
112	78	66
197	80	88
143	93	61
128	143	136
207	158	92

1991

Movie poster for *Slacker*
Artist: Unknown

R	G	B
33	65	141
254	211	0
170	31	35
85	182	128
0	0	0

"SPELLBINDING...A SCRAPPY AND SHREWDLY HILARIOUS FIRST FILM"
—Peter Travers, ROLLING STONE MAGAZINE

"EXHILARATING. THERE IS NOTHING MORE AMUSING,
ORIGINAL OR OUTRAGEOUS ON THE CURRENT MOVIE SCENE."
—David Sterritt, THE CHRISTIAN SCIENCE MONITOR

SLACKER

Written, Produced and Directed by RICHARD LINKLATER
Cameraman LEE DANIEL Production Manager, Casting ANNE WALKER-McBAY Dolly Grip, Assistant Camera CLARK WALKER Sound DENISE MONTGOMERY
Editor SCOTT RHODES Script Supervisor MEG BRENNAN A Detour Filmproduction Cast A LOT OF PEOPLE

An ORION Release
CLASSICS

R RESTRICTED
UNDER 17 REQUIRES ACCOMPANYING
PARENT OR ADULT GUARDIAN

music +style
(the bible of)

PREMIERE ISSUE

rAY GUn

henry rollins
sonic youth
house of love
inspiral carpets
john wesley
harding
the lemonheads
luna
opus 111
the prodigy
mary's danish
mission k
too much joy
david j
matt mahurin

one november 1992
$3.50 u.s. $3.95 canada

1992

Cover for *Ray Gun* magazine
Artist: David Carson

R	G	B
205	170	51
0	0	0
92	18	14
206	196	203
81	90	142

1993

**Montage of central ideas for the Deutsches
Schauspielhaus, Hamburg**

Artist: Neville Brody

R	G	B
82	178	173
215	225	133
130	152	57
168	170	173
84	99	173

Schauspielhaus

Deutsches
Schauspielhaus
in **Hamburg**

(040) 24871-0

BEASTIE BOYS
NORTH AMERICAN TOUR

©1994 T.A.Z.   #123

1994

Poster for the Beastie Boys
North American Tour
Artist: TAZ

R	G	B
0	0	0
255	229	0
158	25	20
30	49	99
211	19	31

1995

Poster for *Army of Me* by Bjork
Artist: Paul White

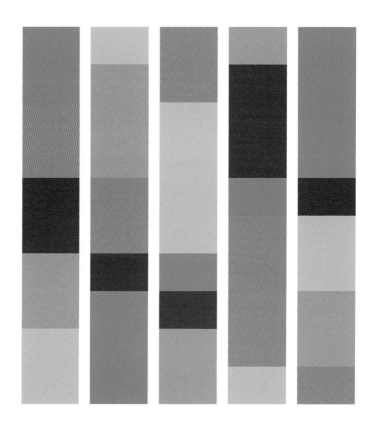

R	G	B
0	145	205
221	125	174
202	20	30
239	146	106
168	198	177

1996

Poster from the series *Morisawa 10*
Artist: John Maeda

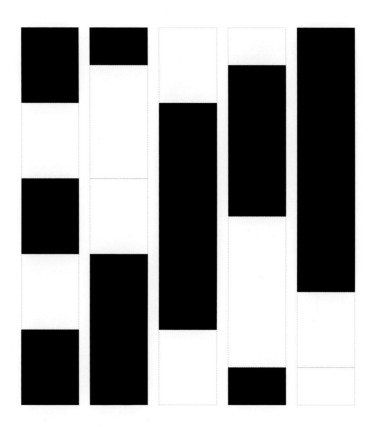

R	G	B
0	0	0
255	255	255
0	0	0
255	255	255
0	0	0

1997

Poster for the Bauhaus program
Artist: Detlef Fielder & Daniela Haufer

R	G	B
206	221	169
152	172	54
174	137	47
242	160	99
221	122	49

stiftung bauhaus dessau juli
august
1997

bauhaus

bis **03.08.97** beständeausstellung
bauhaus 1919 –1933 bauhausgebäude ausstellungsebene
18.07.97 bis 03.08. eröffnung 17.07. 17h
max-klinger-stipendium nordraum
31.08.97 bis 04.01.98 eröffnung 30.08. 18h
gunta stölzl bauhausgebäude ausstellungsebene

und 27.07.
grubenwanderung in golpa-nord 14uhr

bis 07.09. sommerschule 1997
raum ohne eigenschaften

kino in der bauhausaula
accatone 20uhr

kino in der bauhausaula
tee im harem des archimedes 20uhr

kino in der bauhausaula
alphaville 20uhr

1998

Sitcker and poster design
titled *Viva la Posse*
Artist: Shepard Fairey

R	G	B
214	102	29
224	154	21
103	117	41
0	0	0
0	116	134

1999

Exhibition poster for *Objects in Space*
at the American Institute of Graphic Arts
(AIGA), Orange Country
Artist: April Greiman

R	G	B
179	59	141
220	212	128
209	93	45
85	124	45
67	16	21

the eye walks, jumps, journeys through,

it is where relationships are established, not simply communicated.

out side

A sheet of paper isn't merely a

but a field or space that is traversed,

journeys through, inside and outside of

relationships are established, not simply communicated.

objects in space

9

the

au
spi
ci
ous
eiga /
oc

ob
in
sp

9/

9/9/
99/

Gretgarska Legostian
other own marking
(in space of course)

April Greiman
recent

9

		FOGRA 39				US SHEETFED COATED v2				US WEB COATED (SWOP) v2			
		C	M	Y	K	C	M	Y	K	C	M	Y	K
1900		89	56	28	7	87	54	27	7	91	61	21	9
		7	28	73	0	9	24	71	0	9	27	75	0
		2	9	40	0	3	8	33	0	3	8	37	0
		21	42	40	0	22	38	38	1	22	41	40	0
		6	62	63	0	8	61	64	0	10	64	67	0
1901		58	48	73	31	60	49	72	27	55	48	76	29
		58	40	58	14	56	38	57	13	56	40	59	13
		16	47	72	1	16	45	71	2	17	46	75	1
		20	27	33	0	19	24	29	0	18	25	31	0
		42	75	85	57	50	80	87	52	41	75	87	54
1902		22	84	94	13	25	86	85	17	24	87	100	18
		20	50	68	2	21	48	68	5	22	50	71	3
		17	29	45	0	18	25	42	0	18	28	44	0
		35	62	61	16	36	62	63	18	34	63	64	16
		60	44	58	19	60	43	58	17	58	44	59	18
1903		11	25	90	0	15	23	87	0	17	27	93	0
		65	31	68	11	62	30	66	11	64	33	71	13
		81	73	24	8	79	70	29	11	82	78	28	13
		13	92	100	3	18	93	85	8	20	92	100	10
		0	0	0	100	0	0	0	100	0	0	0	100
1904		83	76	50	52	87	80	57	46	78	74	50	52
		42	43	84	33	49	47	85	23	45	47	92	24
		22	70	93	13	24	70	86	13	23	73	100	12
		3	15	28	0	4	12	22	0	3	13	24	0
		27	20	31	3	49	44	60	15	46	44	62	14
1905		26	90	79	21	31	92	77	22	27	91	84	25
		11	38	29	0	14	33	27	0	13	36	29	0
		23	35	44	1	24	31	42	1	23	34	44	0
		15	74	93	3	15	74	85	5	17	77	98	5
		42	69	84	48	48	73	84	42	40	70	87	44
1906		25	6	32	0	17	5	23	0	22	7	30	0
		0	31	34	0	2	22	25	0	2	28	32	0
		1	2	42	0	2	3	31	0	2	2	40	0
		27	8	51	0	19	7	44	0	24	9	51	0
		3	0	15	0	2	1	9	0	2	0	12	0
1907		80	61	24	5	78	59	27	8	82	66	27	9
		28	45	90	6	26	43	85	7	27	44	96	6
		21	85	100	11	22	87	88	13	22	87	100	14
		5	8	24	0	6	8	20	0	5	7	22	0
		0	0	0	100	0	0	0	100	0	0	0	100
1908		28	82	94	24	32	84	87	25	28	84	99	27
		33	46	68	9	31	44	67	9	31	45	72	7
		9	13	25	0	10	12	21	0	8	12	22	0
		37	32	42	1	34	28	38	2	34	31	41	1
		65	61	64	52	71	65	70	47	61	60	66	50
1909		27	91	88	24	31	94	82	25	28	92	94	28
		75	36	96	25	76	38	89	23	74	38	100	28
		72	35	56	12	71	35	55	13	72	37	57	15
		17	52	92	2	19	51	87	6	20	53	96	46
		40	72	73	41	45	75	76	38	38	73	76	40

	FOGRA 39				US SHEETFED COATED v2				US WEB COATED (SWOP) v2			
	C	M	Y	K	C	M	Y	K	C	M	Y	K
1910	1	59	93	0	9	59	87	1	11	62	97	1
	1	35	89	0	8	33	86	0	9	36	91	0
	19	55	100	4	21	55	92	7	22	56	100	6
	5	72	99	1	12	73	89	3	15	75	100	3
	25	90	100	20	29	93	88	22	27	91	100	24
1911	13	91	57	3	14	93	56	2	18	93	65	4
	45	31	67	15	41	28	67	6	45	34	72	8
	75	53	35	22	77	52	33	10	77	58	38	17
	11	65	35	1	12	61	29	0	16	67	37	0
	11	16	23	1	8	11	16	0	10	14	21	0
1912	77	36	77	23	78	38	75	21	76	37	79	26
	28	14	33	0	23	13	27	0	24	13	31	0
	6	37	30	0	11	33	28	0	10	35	29	0
	15	92	100	5	18	93	84	8	19	92	100	9
	52	74	77	76	64	85	90	71	52	72	78	73
1913	3	38	32	0	8	33	30	0	8	36	32	0
	15	77	70	3	19	76	69	7	20	80	75	7
	47	48	46	9	46	46	45	10	44	47	47	8
	11	27	71	0	15	25	70	0	15	28	73	0
	49	32	82	10	48	31	80	11	47	34	87	11
1914	50	49	85	30	53	51	84	27	48	50	90	28
	35	38	76	6	35	36	75	9	34	38	80	7
	15	12	32	0	14	11	27	0	14	12	31	0
	32	81	100	37	38	84	93	36	32	82	100	37
	0	0	0	100	0	0	0	100	0	0	0	100
1915	55	50	59	22	56	50	60	20	52	50	61	21
	47	80	52	36	51	82	61	33	44	81	55	37
	75	46	70	38	78	49	71	33	73	46	72	38
	45	36	84	11	44	35	81	12	44	37	89	11
	15	13	64	0	16	14	62	0	18	16	66	0
1916	26	43	92	5	27	41	88	7	27	43	97	6
	37	59	96	27	40	60	91	26	36	60	100	26
	71	72	48	40	74	75	54	35	68	72	48	40
	24	32	54	1	24	29	53	2	24	32	56	0
	26	87	96	21	30	90	86	24	27	88	100	25
1917	51	51	94	34	54	53	90	31	49	52	100	32
	39	56	99	25	41	56	93	25	38	56	100	25
	27	38	76	3	27	36	75	5	27	38	80	3
	65	53	56	29	67	54	58	25	62	53	57	28
	26	66	96	14	28	67	89	16	27	68	100	16
1918	44	49	61	16	44	49	62	16	42	49	64	15
	74	54	31	8	73	53	32	10	75	57	33	11
	23	62	100	8	25	62	91	12	25	64	100	11
	52	29	46	2	48	26	43	4	50	29	46	2
	90	70	44	35	92	72	50	31	88	72	45	37
1919	18	85	90	7	16	87	91	6	20	87	97	10
	15	23	49	2	15	16	45	0	18	22	53	0
	22	68	80	12	20	67	82	8	23	71	85	11
	53	33	51	17	49	30	49	6	54	36	55	9
	53	65	40	32	55	66	42	15	55	69	45	24

		FOGRA 39				US SHEETFED COATED v2				US WEB COATED (SWOP) v2			
		C	M	Y	K	C	M	Y	K	C	M	Y	K
1920		66	57	43	18	66	57	44	17	64	58	43	19
		51	22	70	2	47	22	67	4	49	25	74	4
		7	13	75	0	8	12	73	0	9	14	77	0
		16	59	86	2	18	58	82	6	19	60	89	5
		15	87	91	5	19	88	82	10	21	89	97	11
1921		48	95	29	26	51	97	36	13	49	96	40	24
		57	22	56	2	53	22	54	4	56	25	58	3
		4	13	28	0	6	12	24	0	5	12	25	0
		42	82	84	65	52	90	90	60	42	80	85	62
		0	59	87	0	3	55	88	0	3	55	88	0
1922		67	93	44	49	71	96	56	45	61	89	47	51
		15	91	65	3	20	91	65	7	21	92	73	9
		26	94	93	22	31	97	84	24	27	94	99	27
		16	21	73	0	18	20	72	0	20	23	76	0
		50	33	26	1	46	30	25	1	48	33	27	0
1923		6	68	84	0	12	68	80	2	14	71	88	2
		100	93	36	31	100	89	48	31	96	90	40	38
		8	38	21	0	19	88	70	7	20	89	78	9
		39	69	30	3	39	67	33	7	39	72	34	5
		15	22	20	0	14	18	18	0	13	20	18	0
1924		4	81	42	0	13	80	47	1	16	84	51	2
		80	62	11	1	78	60	18	3	83	69	18	3
		7	11	75	0	11	12	72	0	12	15	76	0
		7	46	79	0	12	44	78	1	13	46	82	0
		67	27	73	8	64	27	70	9	67	29	76	11
1925		29	51	0	0	30	47	9	0	31	51	7	0
		56	68	5	0	55	65	16	2	59	73	15	1
		17	59	68	2	19	58	68	5	20	60	72	4
		7	33	82	0	13	30	80	0	14	33	85	0
		53	23	65	2	49	22	62	4	51	25	68	4
1926		55	6	52	0	47	6	46	0	53	11	53	0
		42	66	0	0	38	62	0	0	42	69	7	0
		2	8	28	0	2	5	19	0	2	7	25	0
		0	44	50	0	3	36	43	0	4	42	50	0
		91	78	62	97	95	85	84	84	75	68	67	89
1927		100	90	29	16	100	85	38	20	99	91	34	25
		21	93	100	11	24	95	86	16	24	93	100	18
		0	0	0	100	0	0	0	100	0	0	0	100
		31	25	18	0	27	21	17	0	27	23	16	0
		2	2	0	0	2	2	0	0	1	1	0	0
1928		4	56	4	0	12	52	13	0	13	56	11	0
		100	92	17	4	99	85	28	11	100	93	28	15
		45	3	50	0	40	7	47	0	44	10	52	0
		74	45	11	0	71	44	16	2	77	51	18	1
		35	54	86	19	37	55	84	19	35	55	91	19
1929		26	86	86	23	27	86	86	23	27	86	86	23
		15	28	80	0	15	28	79	0	15	29	80	0
		17	44	82	1	17	44	82	1	18	45	83	2
		91	70	52	51	91	69	52	51	91	70	52	52
		64	40	40	7	63	41	40	7	63	41	40	7

Year	FOGRA 39				US SHEETFED COATED v2				US WEB COATED (SWOP) v2			
	C	M	Y	K	C	M	Y	K	C	M	Y	K
1930	32	41	71	6	32	39	71	8	31	41	75	6
	5	27	85	0	11	25	82	0	12	28	87	0
	33	91	100	48	40	96	93	45	33	89	100	47
	69	45	67	29	71	46	67	26	67	45	69	29
	19	92	52	3	23	92	56	8	24	93	60	10
1931	74	75	48	56	70	75	52	53	70	75	52	53
	49	47	44	33	55	53	51	19	54	53	51	19
	73	37	51	26	75	42	55	20	75	42	55	20
	51	24	37	6	50	27	38	1	50	27	38	1
	47	53	27	9	47	55	30	3	48	55	30	4
1932	85	71	44	34	87	73	50	0	83	72	44	36
	89	70	35	19	90	69	40	20	89	74	37	24
	60	38	27	1	56	36	26	3	60	39	28	2
	25	18	27	0	22	16	24	0	21	17	25	0
	6	19	88	0	11	19	85	0	13	22	89	0
1933	71	67	64	73	82	78	75	68	67	66	66	71
	41	36	31	1	38	33	29	1	38	35	30	0
	99	87	28	15	99	83	36	19	98	89	33	24
	39	47	77	15	40	46	77	16	38	47	81	15
	15	18	28	0	15	16	24	0	14	16	26	0
1934	4	91	88	0	19	91	80	9	20	91	95	11
	0	61	83	0	13	71	83	3	15	75	93	3
	24	49	87	16	38	68	92	28	33	68	100	29
	63	15	77	1	64	36	81	19	62	37	89	22
	7	4	8	0	7	4	7	0	5	3	5	0
1935	41	15	38	0	36	15	34	0	38	17	38	0
	5	68	54	0	13	67	56	2	15	71	58	1
	26	89	73	19	30	91	73	20	27	91	78	23
	4	35	8	0	8	28	11	0	7	32	9	0
	0	0	0	100	0	0	0	100	0	0	0	100
1936	79	52	0	0	76	51	11	0	83	61	11	1
	100	92	39	56	100	95	58	49	91	87	47	56
	75	43	32	5	73	43	32	7	76	47	34	7
	30	27	57	1	29	24	55	2	29	27	59	0
	16	56	57	1	19	55	57	4	19	57	60	2
1937	5	14	24	0	6	12	20	0	5	13	21	0
	33	55	70	13	34	54	70	15	32	56	74	14
	46	26	66	3	43	24	64	5	44	27	69	4
	55	33	52	6	52	31	50	7	53	33	53	6
	5	85	100	1	13	85	86	4	16	87	100	5
1938	12	22	61	0	14	20	60	0	15	23	63	0
	39	59	52	13	49	58	53	15	38	60	53	13
	20	30	51	0	20	27	49	1	20	29	52	0
	49	53	75	31	52	55	76	28	46	53	78	29
	68	59	72	65	77	65	78	58	64	58	73	62
1939	8	5	83	0	12	8	79	0	13	11	84	0
	53	25	83	5	50	25	79	7	52	28	87	7
	64	37	24	1	60	35	24	2	65	40	26	2
	0	88	93	0	10	89	82	2	13	91	100	3
	2	71	73	0	11	71	73	2	13	74	78	2

		FOGRA 39				US SHEETFED COATED v2				US WEB COATED (SWOP) v2			
		C	M	Y	K	C	M	Y	K	C	M	Y	K
1940		73	54	74	59	80	59	78	52	69	54	75	57
		70	37	76	22	71	38	74	20	69	38	79	24
		17	21	52	0	18	20	49	0	18	22	53	0
		6	89	53	0	15	89	57	3	17	91	62	4
		22	93	64	9	25	93	65	14	25	93	71	16
1941		44	44	99	19	44	43	92	18	42	44	100	18
		16	42	66	1	16	39	65	2	16	41	69	1
		3	5	12	0	4	4	10	0	2	4	9	0
		14	87	100	3	15	89	86	5	17	89	100	7
		68	35	26	1	62	31	24	2	68	36	26	1
1942		100	96	33	29	100	91	47	29	96	93	38	36
		78	68	14	1	76	65	20	5	80	74	21	5
		63	46	76	33	65	48	76	29	60	46	78	33
		5	14	83	0	10	15	80	0	11	17	84	0
		27	89	82	22	31	91	79	23	27	90	87	26
1943		21	34	96	1	22	32	91	3	24	35	100	2
		61	45	89	33	64	47	85	29	58	45	93	33
		37	39	73	8	37	37	73	10	36	39	77	8
		50	46	73	22	51	46	73	21	47	46	76	21
		81	52	55	32	84	54	57	28	80	53	55	33
1944		80	47	0	0	78	47	10	0	84	56	11	0
		55	87	44	33	57	89	53	31	52	87	47	36
		58	46	36	6	56	44	35	7	57	46	36	6
		27	26	37	0	25	23	33	0	24	25	36	0
		40	55	57	15	41	55	58	16	38	55	59	15
1945		100	94	35	29	100	90	47	29	96	91	38	36
		46	29	35	1	42	26	32	1	43	29	34	0
		18	49	39	1	21	46	38	1	22	49	40	0
		42	79	77	59	50	85	84	55	40	78	80	56
		14	88	96	3	18	89	84	98	20	90	100	10
1946		82	37	39	6	80	37	37	8	84	42	40	10
		90	55	28	7	89	55	29	9	92	62	31	11
		97	25	85	10	87	29	78	15	88	31	86	20
		75	15	91	2	72	18	85	5	76	22	97	7
		0	0	0	100	0	0	0	100	0	0	0	100
1947		57	22	79	3	53	22	76	6	56	25	83	6
		76	71	26	9	75	69	30	11	77	75	29	13
		5	26	62	0	10	23	61	0	10	26	64	0
		15	79	91	4	19	79	82	8	20	82	97	9
		27	87	100	25	32	90	89	27	28	88	100	28
1948		77	73	56	67	85	84	65	61	72	71	58	66
		72	69	47	35	75	71	52	31	69	69	47	36
		14	72	100	2	17	72	89	7	19	74	100	7
		1	16	78	0	7	16	75	0	8	18	79	0
		0	89	99	0	10	91	85	2	14	91	100	4
1949		18	91	48	2	23	91	53	7	24	92	56	8
		67	47	17	1	64	45	20	2	69	51	21	2
		49	10	54	0	44	13	51	0	48	16	56	0
		92	75	53	64	98	84	62	58	85	72	55	64
		13	19	79	0	16	19	77	0	18	22	82	0

	FOGRA 39				US SHEETFED COATED v2				US WEB COATED (SWOP) v2			
	C	M	Y	K	C	M	Y	K	C	M	Y	K
1950	7	41	31	0	11	37	29	0	11	39	31	0
	64	36	36	4	61	34	34	5	64	38	37	4
	68	64	31	10	66	62	33	11	68	67	33	13
	72	22	58	3	68	23	55	5	73	26	61	7
	14	15	36	0	14	14	31	0	13	15	35	0
1951	36	46	76	12	36	45	76	13	35	46	80	12
	42	31	71	4	40	29	70	7	40	31	74	5
	24	19	29	0	21	16	25	0	21	18	27	0
	10	14	26	0	11	13	22	0	9	13	24	0
	25	18	51	0	24	17	48	0	24	19	52	0
1952	29	99	91	12	22	100	90	14	24	98	95	20
	85	54	51	51	92	59	56	31	86	60	56	45
	0	8	45	0	2	6	35	0	2	7	43	0
	12	70	76	2	11	68	75	2	15	73	80	3
	34	7	41	0	24	6	33	0	31	9	40	0
1953	100	95	40	41	100	89	47	29	94	90	42	45
	69	27	78	10	65	22	78	7	69	29	82	12
	6	0	66	0	5	2	58	0	7	2	67	0
	40	38	20	4	33	31	15	0	38	38	21	0
	15	14	45	1	11	11	36	0	14	14	44	0
1954	7	36	87	0	7	29	89	0	10	36	91	0
	14	4	89	0	11	5	89	0	15	7	92	0
	6	66	16	0	9	62	12	0	11	67	20	0
	62	8	36	0	55	8	29	0	61	13	36	0
	4	14	19	0	3	9	13	0	4	12	16	0
1955	75	66	64	85	83	73	78	69	71	65	68	80
	89	64	38	29	93	64	37	16	90	69	41	27
	71	70	47	51	76	73	52	32	70	72	51	46
	26	45	100	18	26	42	100	8	31	48	100	10
	14	11	23	0	9	7	15	0	11	9	20	0
1956	42	40	56	26	49	44	60	15	46	44	62	14
	13	9	67	0	12	9	64	0	13	11	69	0
	40	15	55	1	35	15	52	0	37	17	56	0
	6	66	32	0	9	64	34	0	11	67	35	0
	4	82	69	0	7	83	68	0	11	86	75	1
1957	11	8	66	0	9	33	86	0	10	36	91	0
	80	44	68	49	12	4	87	0	15	7	92	0
	15	69	67	3	9	62	20	0	11	67	20	0
	13	96	87	3	54	9	31	0	61	13	36	0
	98	69	33	20	5	12	16	0	4	12	16	0
1958	0	0	0	100	0	0	0	100	0	0	0	100
	1	96	96	0	5	98	82	0	11	97	100	2
	77	11	100	1	73	12	93	2	78	18	100	4
	69	18	0	0	61	16	1	0	69	24	4	0
	9	1	86	0	8	1	84	0	11	4	88	0
1959	7	13	89	0	8	12	87	0	9	14	92	0
	61	71	28	12	59	69	32	10	60	75	31	11
	62	3	72	0	55	4	68	0	62	10	76	0
	9	83	95	1	11	84	84	2	14	86	100	4
	7	60	56	1	9	59	56	0	11	62	58	0

	FOGRA 39				US SHEETFED COATED v2				US WEB COATED (SWOP) v2			
	C	M	Y	K	C	M	Y	K	C	M	Y	K
1960	99	96	24	13	98	91	33	15	98	97	30	19
	85	83	15	3	83	78	20	5	87	88	20	6
	40	46	25	7	40	45	26	2	40	47	27	1
	5	63	85	0	7	63	82	0	9	65	89	0
	33	74	84	41	40	77	84	35	34	76	89	36
1961	5	48	78	0	6	42	78	0	9	48	82	0
	84	27	92	13	83	24	93	11	84	29	98	17
	83	34	26	0	85	34	23	2	86	42	29	4
	17	83	11	0	17	85	11	0	23	87	22	0
	0	0	0	100	0	0	0	100	0	0	0	100
1962	50	13	6	0	41	12	6	0	45	15	6	0
	0	0	0	100	0	0	0	100	0	0	0	100
	13	3	69	0	11	4	66	0	13	5	71	0
	10	81	70	2	12	81	69	2	15	84	76	3
	64	83	20	6	60	80	26	7	64	87	25	9
1963	9	90	87	2	11	92	79	3	15	93	96	4
	89	77	33	21	89	76	37	18	89	81	35	23
	4	44	10	0	7	38	12	0	7	41	10	0
	9	82	46	1	11	82	49	1	15	86	53	1
	9	6	88	0	9	6	86	0	11	9	91	0
1964	75	27	27	7	75	26	24	1	78	34	30	2
	64	18	28	2	59	16	23	0	64	23	29	0
	37	15	60	2	29	13	56	0	35	18	63	0
	58	32	83	17	53	28	85	11	57	34	88	15
	85	27	60	13	86	25	58	9	87	32	63	14
1965	9	73	93	1	11	73	85	2	13	76	99	25
	10	34	89	1	12	31	87	0	14	34	94	0
	12	19	84	1	13	18	85	0	15	20	87	0
	48	38	33	15	50	40	36	5	50	41	37	4
	14	72	41	3	16	71	44	2	19	75	45	2
1966	14	94	79	4	15	96	73	5	18	95	87	7
	70	22	20	2	64	21	19	0	71	27	22	0
	5	21	74	0	6	18	73	0	7	21	76	0
	85	54	24	8	84	53	25	7	88	61	27	7
	53	6	83	0	46	6	80	0	52	11	89	0
1967	8	88	98	1	19	90	85	2	14	91	100	4
	86	100	9	2	83	96	20	5	87	100	20	7
	35	52	99	38	44	57	96	27	40	56	100	28
	55	93	31	28	57	93	44	22	54	94	39	27
	29	26	78	9	30	26	78	4	31	30	84	2
1968	76	81	23	8	73	77	27	96	76	85	26	11
	91	74	14	2	88	69	18	4	93	81	18	4
	81	45	31	15	81	47	33	9	84	52	34	11
	8	85	82	1	10	86	77	2	13	88	89	3
	16	33	73	5	19	31	73	28	20	34	77	0
1969	7	15	78	0	8	14	76	0	9	16	80	0
	22	77	85	12	23	78	81	13	23	80	91	13
	63	66	38	28	65	68	44	21	64	69	41	23
	73	27	16	2	68	26	16	0	75	33	18	0
	19	65	34	5	22	64	37	2	24	68	38	1

		FOGRA 39				US SHEETFED COATED v2				US WEB COATED (SWOP) v2		
	C	M	Y	K	C	M	Y	K	C	M	Y	K
1970	11	95	21	1	13	96	31	0	19	97	34	1
	17	4	83	0	15	4	81	0	16	7	86	0
	8	92	89	1	10	95	80	2	14	94	98	4
	62	6	78	0	55	7	74	0	62	13	83	1
	50	17	4	0	41	15	5	0	45	18	5	0
1971	12	24	15	0	11	19	15	0	10	21	13	0
	21	99	97	14	24	99	84	15	24	98	100	17
	22	81	18	2	24	80	25	1	27	85	27	1
	42	93	36	45	52	96	56	33	45	94	50	38
	34	55	10	0	31	50	13	0	33	55	12	0
1972	14	6	77	0	13	6	74	0	14	8	79	0
	85	49	30	14	85	50	30	9	88	56	33	11
	10	65	82	1	12	65	79	2	13	68	86	2
	28	77	85	27	27	78	89	18	29	80	91	25
	60	6	84	0	53	7	79	0	59	13	89	1
1973	0	0	0	100	0	0	0	100	0	0	0	100
	6	52	73	0	8	51	73	0	9	53	77	0
	11	3	67	0	9	4	64	0	11	5	69	0
	0	0	0	0	0	0	0	0	0	0	0	0
	16	84	10	0	17	82	19	0	22	87	21	0
1974	.27	67	22	3	28	64	26	2	29	70	27	1
	50	20	58	3	46	19	56	2	49	22	61	2
	10	14	27	0	10	12	22	0	9	12	24	0
	23	59	79	14	25	59	78	11	25	61	85	10
	58	43	20	4	55	40	20	2	58	44	22	1
1975	14	93	97	4	15	95	84	6	18	94	100	7
	31	62	74	32	39	65	77	24	34	65	80	25
	19	30	85	7	22	29	85	2	23	32	91	1
	0	0	0	100	0	0	0	100	0	0	0	100
	86	45	22	6	85	44	22	4	89	52	25	4
1976	100	87	16	3	99	81	23	7	100	92	23	9
	55	74	8	0	51	70	14	1	56	78	14	1
	7	11	85	0	7	11	84	0	9	13	87	0
	6	29	90	0	8	25	89	0	9	29	93	0
	8	93	85	1	10	96	77	2	14	95	94	4
1977	0	76	25	0	5	75	21	0	8	78	31	0
	87	76	62	94	94	83	82	82	75	68	66	88
	0	74	74	0	4	73	73	0	7	77	79	0
	19	11	62	1	15	9	57	0	18	13	64	0
	83	55	12	1	84	51	9	0	85	61	15	2
1978	52	12	14	0	44	12	13	0	49	15	14	0
	41	5	52	0	35	6	47	0	38	9	52	0
	16	4	68	0	14	4	64	0	15	5	69	0
	7	54	63	0	9	51	63	0	11	54	66	0
	14	57	21	1	15	53	23	0	16	57	23	0
1979	15	3	63	0	13	4	59	0	15	5	64	0
	7	74	81	1	9	75	78	1	12	77	87	2
	67	21	15	1	60	20	14	0	67	26	16	0
	56	5	68	0	49	7	65	0	15	11	73	0
	9	82	32	1	12	81	36	0	16	85	38	1

Year	FOGRA 39				US SHEETFED COATED v2				US WEB COATED (SWOP) v2			
	C	M	Y	K	C	M	Y	K	C	M	Y	K
1980	60	49	26	9	58	47	27	5	61	51	28	4
	43	20	20	2	37	18	19	0	40	20	20	0
	51	16	56	2	45	16	53	1	49	19	58	1
	13	16	61	1	13	15	59	0	13	16	62	0
	14	36	34	3	16	32	32	0	16	35	33	0
1981	20	96	87	11	22	98	78	12	22	97	96	14
	49	71	7	0	45	67	13	0	49	75	13	0
	91	74	7	1	89	69	13	2	93	82	14	2
	62	7	16	0	53	7	15	0	61	13	17	0
	82	29	59	14	81	29	58	11	84	33	62	14
1982	13	3	66	0	11	4	62	0	13	5	67	0
	64	18	30	2	58	18	27	0	64	22	31	0
	19	87	13	1	20	85	22	0	25	91	24	0
	96	92	8	1	95	86	18	5	98	97	18	5
	11	24	70	1	13	22	69	0	13	24	73	0
1983	12	50	36	2	14	46	35	0	15	49	36	0
	10	36	84	1	12	33	83	0	13	35	88	0
	43	31	39	12	45	32	40	4	45	34	42	2
	72	62	16	2	68	58	19	4	73	66	19	3
	24	76	87	16	26	77	82	16	25	79	93	16
1984	12	24	91	2	13	22	90	0	15	24	95	0
	8	79	70	1	10	79	69	2	13	82	76	2
	72	45	85	45	77	49	82	38	70	46	87	43
	23	83	20	3	24	83	28	2	28	87	29	2
	93	90	7	1	92	84	16	4	95	96	17	5
1985	21	95	87	13	23	97	79	13	23	96	95	15
	80	28	71	13	78	27	68	11	80	30	75	15
	0	0	0	100	0	0	0	100	0	0	0	100
	86	68	9	0	84	64	14	2	89	75	14	2
	12	17	23	1	12	15	20	0	11	15	21	0
1986	16	3	64	0	13	4	61	0	15	5	65	0
	73	16	58	2	68	16	55	2	74	20	61	3
	59	94	27	18	59	93	38	16	58	95	34	20
	65	24	14	1	59	22	15	0	65	28	16	0
	10	98	86	2	12	98	76	48	15	99	95	5
1987	12	92	36	2	15	93	42	1	19	95	45	2
	0	0	0	100	0	0	0	100	0	0	0	100
	10	4	79	0	9	4	76	0	11	6	80	0
	97	75	10	1	96	70	16	3	99	83	17	4
	1	61	73	0	4	56	71	0	7	62	77	0
1988	29	100	73	36	36	100	7	31	30	99	80	34
	13	32	86	2	14	29	85	1	16	33	91	0
	0	0	0	100	0	0	0	100	0	0	0	100
	88	100	30	29	88	97	42	27	85	97	36	32
	17	13	14	0	15	11	13	0	14	11	11	0
1989	0	0	0	100	0	0	0	100	0	0	0	100
	9	88	55	1	11	89	57	2	15	91	62	2
	6	52	74	0	8	50	74	0	10	53	78	0
	86	46	19	4	84	44	20	3	89	52	22	3
	70	13	90	1	64	13	85	2	71	18	98	3

Year	FOGRA 39 C	M	Y	K	US SHEETFED COATED v2 C	M	Y	K	US WEB COATED (SWOP) v2 C	M	Y	K
1990	38	58	58	48	51	65	69	33	45	64	67	35
	20	78	56	10	23	78	59	8	23	81	62	9
	32	59	72	33	40	62	76	25	36	62	78	25
	52	32	42	14	53	33	42	6	54	36	45	5
	19	39	68	8	22	37	69	4	23	40	73	2
1991	99	82	15	3	99	76	21	6	100	88	22	7
	7	18	90	0	8	16	89	0	9	18	93	0
	24	97	86	21	28	98	80	20	25	97	95	22
	68	6	63	0	62	7	60	0	69	13	67	1
	0	0	0	100	0	0	0	100	0	0	0	100
1992	22	29	86	8	25	29	86	3	26	32	93	2
	0	0	0	100	0	0	0	100	0	0	0	100
	37	99	88	61	47	100	87	57	36	93	89	58
	23	23	16	1	20	19	15	0	19	21	14	0
	79	67	22	6	76	64	25	7	80	72	24	7
1993	67	12	39	0	61	12	34	0	68	17	40	0
	25	4	59	0	20	4	56	0	22	6	60	0
	56	26	91	9	53	24	87	8	55	28	98	8
	37	28	26	6	35	27	26	0	36	29	27	0
	66	41	93	35	69	43	87	28	65	42	98	32
1994	0	0	0	100	0	0	0	100	0	0	0	100
	8	7	88	0	8	7	86	0	10	9	90	0
	26	99	98	26	31	100	86	25	27	98	100	27
	100	87	33	24	100	83	40	22	98	88	36	28
	15	98	91	5	16	99	78	7	18	99	99	9
1995	80	34	9	0	75	31	9	0	82	40	12	0
	18	63	9	0	18	60	14	0	64	20	13	0
	17	99	92	8	19	99	79	9	20	99	100	11
	7	53	60	1	9	51	60	0	11	53	62	0
	41	12	36	1	35	12	32	0	38	13	36	0
1996	0	0	0	100	0	0	0	100	0	0	0	100
	0	0	0	0	0	0	0	0	0	0	0	0
	0	0	0	100	0	0	0	100	0	0	0	100
	0	0	0	0	0	0	0	0	0	0	0	0
	0	0	0	100	0	0	0	100	0	0	0	100
1997	27	5	43	0	22	6	38	0	24	7	42	0
	49	19	91	4	45	18	87	3	48	22	97	3
	28	39	87	19	34	41	87	11	33	43	96	9
	6	46	65	0	9	44	64	0	9	45	67	0
	14	60	85	3	15	60	83	4	16	22	90	3
1998	16	68	95	4	16	68	87	5	18	71	100	5
	14	44	94	3	15	42	91	3	18	44	100	1
	61	36	97	25	62	37	92	20	60	38	100	23
	0	0	0	100	0	0	0	100	0	0	0	100
	85	36	37	20	87	40	39	11	89	45	42	13
1999	39	88	10	1	36	86	19	2	41	91	21	26
	21	12	60	1	19	12	57	0	20	13	61	0
	17	72	86	6	18	73	81	7	19	75	92	7
	70	32	99	19	70	31	92	16	69	34	100	20
	45	93	68	74	60	98	80	68	45	85	71	71

PICTURE CREDITS & THANKS

Agence eureka: 130

akg-images: 144; © Les Arts Décoratifs, Paris: 12, 93.

Bridgeman Images/DaTo Images: 108; The Stapleton Collection: 67; Victoria & Albert Museum: 64.

© Neville Brody: 217.

Courtesy Sarah Campbell and Allan Edwards; *Havana*, 1983, original painting by Susan Collier and Sarah Campbell (gouache on paper) for the furnishing fabric collection "Six Views," licensed for production to Christian Fischbacher: 195.

Courtesy David Carson: 214.

Courtesy Seymour Chwast: 188.

Corbis/Christie's Images: 151; K.J. Historical: 207.

Courtesy and © cyan, www.cyan.de: 225.

Courtesy and © Georgina von Etzdorf: 210.

© Jim Evans aka TAZ, www.tazposters.com: 178, 218.

Shepard Fairey/OBEYGIANT. COM: 226.

Getty Images/Galerie Bilderwelt: 71;

Imagno: 37; John D. Kisch/Separate Cinema Archive: 86, 104, 173, 196; Movie Poster Image Art: 119, 133, 81, 147; Museum of London/Heritage Images: 41; Print Collector: 34, 155, 163; SSPL: 126.

© Milton Glaser: 160.

April Greiman/made in space: 203, 229.

Images Musicales collection, www.imagesmusicales.be: 59.

Library & Archives Canada: 78

Library of Congress, Washington, D.C.: 15, 19, 28, 31, 38, 42, 46, 49, 90, 94, 107.

Courtesy John Maeda: 222.

MAK – Austrian Museum of Applied Arts/Contemporary Art: Photo: © MAK: 27; Photo: © MAK/Ingrid Schindler: 20.

Mary Evans Picture Library: 75, 116; Museum of Domestic Design & Architecture (MODA): 89; The National Army Museum: 103.

Me Company 1995. www.mecompany.com: 221.

Courtesy of New Order and Peter Saville: 204.

Photofest © Orion Pictures: 213.

Private Collection: 24, 45, 53, 63, 68, 72, 85, 97, 100, 111, 115, 122, 129, 134, 138, 148, 156, 170, 174, 182, 192, 199, 200.

© Simon Rendall: 56.

Rex/Courtesy Everett Collection: 137, 141.

Scala, Florence: 16; Cooper-Hewitt, National Design Museum, Smithsonian Institution/Art Resource, NY: 112, 210; Digital image, The Museum of Modern Art, New York: 185, 191, 204.

© Victoria and Albert Museum, London: 50, 125, 152, 169, 195.

Courtesy of Wolfgang's Vault (www.wolfgangsvault.com) © Wolfgang's Vault: 159, 177.

Every effort has been made to credit the images and contact copyright holders where known. However, the publisher apologizes for any omissions and welcomes additional information.

Acknowledgments

Thanks go to everyone who helped make this book, in particular Ellie Wilson for her endless patience and support. To all at Ilex: Zara Larcombe for inviting me to work on the project, Frank Gallagher and Julie Weir for making it all happen, and Richard Wolfströme for the creative layouts. For permission to feature such inspirational work, huge appreciation goes to: Jim Evans, April Greiman, John Maeda and Marina Mikhalis, David Carson, Neville Brody, Peter Saville and Alice Cowling, Milton Glaser and Dan Bates, Seymour Chwast, Paul White and Jonathan Tobin at Me Company, Detlef Fielder and Daniela Haufer at cyan, Georgina von Etzdorf and Jimmy Docherty, Sarah Campbell and Allan Edwards, Simon Rendall, Shepard Fairey and Vanthi Pham at OBEY.

For supplying images and advice, thanks to: Frank and Divine Lateur-Crappé at Images Musicales, Valentina Bandelloni at Scala, Olivia Stroud at V&A Images, Thomas Matyk at MAK, Holly Taylor at Bridgeman, and Mark Vivian at Mary Evans, and to all of the collections that proved to be such a great resource.

To every artist and designer, known and unknown, whose work appears within these pages—thank you for making the 20th century more colorful.